MW01709051

résumé rescue

ESSENTIAL RÉSUMÉ SAVING TECHNIQUES

BARBARA J. BOWES FCHRP, CMC

I wanted to take this opportunity to thank you for writing the "best and most practical" resume writing tool in the marketplace. I have been using your methodology for over 10 years, and the feedback from all levels of individuals and corporate clients has been outstanding.

— Fiorella Callocchia, CHRP *President, HR IMPACT*

ISBN 978-2-923653-18-1

Legal Deposit 2010, Library and Archives Canada

Published in Winnipeg, Manitoba, by Vidacom Inc.
Send email to vidacom@mts.net

Résumé Rescue can be purchased through
our website at www.legacybowes.com.
Or call our office at 1-204-947-5525.

Legacy Bowes Group
301-161 Portage Avenue East
Winnipeg Manitoba
R3B 2L6

Acknowledgements

Writing a book under any conditions is difficult. It takes tenacity and persistence. Although I loved teaching my résumé style methodology, writing it down and publishing a book is another thing. So my first book in 1995 was the result of persistent pushing by friends, colleagues and clients.

Since then, the book has been republished three times. I wasn't going to publish it again. However, the continued demand and the compliments I receive suggest that it is still a popular and needed resource. Employment counsellors and career transition professionals tell me that their clients find the process inspiring and uplifting. As a result, their clients gain a new sense of self confidence that appeals to employers and results in the attainment of new jobs. The book is also popular with high school and vocational teachers as they help students move out into the workforce.

From a client perspective, the emails, letters and compliments received suggest this résumé style lifts people's self esteem and confidence and helps to drive them toward success.

So, once again, a special thanks for the "push" from colleagues, friends and clients on republishing this forth edition. It is encouraging to know that my book has had such a positive influence in people's lives.

contents

About the Author

Barbara is President of Legacy Bowes Group and is a leading and most respected authority on human resources. She is a Certified Management Consultant, (CMC), a Certified Human Resource Management Professional (CHRP– Fellow) and holds a Master of Administration in Education. Barbara is also certified in a number of human resource and proprietary operational strategies and has earned the professional level in the Canadian National Speakers Association (CAPS).

Barbara has developed a reputation as the "résumé and interview guru" and a specialist in career management. She has written a weekly column on career issues for the past decade. According to a recent reader survey, Barbara's "Working World" column, is one of the most widely read sections of her local newspaper. In addition, Barbara is also host of a weekly one hour radio show called, *BowesKnows.* Finally, Barbara is in the process of compiling several books which represent a collection of articles from her column, and is also writing a book on leadership.

Barbara has also been active as a community leader. For four years, she was the Founding Chair of the Enterprising Women's Conference, a successful scholarship fundraising event for young women students at a local college. She has also served as President and past president of her local Human Resource Management Association and a past executive member of a Women Business Owners group. Earlier in her career, Barbara served on the Board of the Victorian Order of Nurses, the United Way Board and was an elected school trustee.

Barbara has been nominated and has won numerous awards. Her company was twice a finalist in the Chamber of Commerce Business Awards and she was awarded recognition as one of five "most beautiful women" in her community by a local women's magazine.

Finally, Barbara is a popular motivational guest speaker and workshop leader who can inspire a variety of audiences. Barbara speaks on topics such as human resources, career management, women in leadership and leadership effectiveness.

Why Another Résumé Book?

Why is it that job search candidate's don't make the "first cut" in the résumé review and are never called in for the interview? It's because of a poor résumé. But why rewrite and republish this book on a skills based résumé? The answer is simply because in my view, this book is still the best in the market!

The reason this book is the best is that it focuses on one and one only résumé style. There will be no confusion about what résumé style best suits what industry. And not only that, as you learn and begin to identify your skills and accomplishments, your self esteem will increase to such a level, your friends will have to pull you off the wall!

Most people take themselves for granted. They do their job or tasks so well that they forget how they do them. Not only that, most people fail to credit themselves with the skills they have learned and applied in their volunteer work or from simply being a parent. How many of you hold volunteer roles in your community? How many mothers and fathers need to really apply time management as they drive their kids to all their activities? These tasks require skills too!

The skills based résumé is a valuable strategy to help job candidates with trouble spots, especially when candidate education is outdated or incomplete or for that matter, you are a graduate of the "school of hard knocks" instead of a recognized college or university. This résumé style enables you to value your lifetime experience and to include them in your job marketing campaign.

The skills based résumé is a marketing and sales tool. As such, we recommend that you feel free to place the different information pieces on education, work history, community or professional leadership in any order that best sells what you have to offer. After all, the résumé is your personal masterpiece and you need to concentrate on marketing your strengths not your challenge areas.

Finally, the résumé book is essentially a dictionary of skill-words and phrases that can be recycled. These words and phrases will spark ideas for your own résumé. Select parts of the phrases that apply to you and create a statement that sells your skills.

This résumé style was designed in 1981 and has been used consistently since then. It was designed before the word *competencies* was popular or even known for that matter. Since then, it has been used by career practitioners, teachers, employment counsellors and individuals from all industry sectors as well as high school and university graduates, and mothers who are returning to work.

People who have used this résumé style have been overjoyed by their success. **Why? Because people get interviews and get jobs!** Not only that, their self-esteem soars sky high!

As the author, I am confident this résumé style will bring success to you as well.

Good luck!

Building Your Skills Based Résumé

Researching, preparing for and writing your résumé will not be easy. It will take a good solid effort on your part. A résumé is really an in-depth exploration of yourself and your work. You will have to look very closely at yourself. This requires personal honesty and persistence. If you work steadily on a full time basis, you might have a first draft in two days. If you are working on the résumé part-time, then give yourself at least one week of working every night.

Let's Begin

The steps that you take to create your résumé are systematic and will build on each other as you continue toward the goal. It may appear that we are tackling this project backwards but we are really asking you to do the easy work first. The steps that you will follow are outlined below:

Steps one through five will be repeated with every job (paid or non-paid) that you have had so prepare yourself with extra paper and be prepared for a whole lot of work.

Documenting History

01. Work history
02. Your preferred work environment
03. Education/professional development
04. Professional leadership

Assessing Yourself

05. Your professional expertise/skills

Putting It all Together

06. Developing your personal profile
07. Identifying your accomplishments
08. Finalizing your résumé
    Ordering Key Résumé Components

Documenting History

01. Work History

The first step in building the skills résumé is to assess your work history. The work history assessment includes an examination of all your job titles, all of the activities that make up these jobs, as well as looking at the working environment that surrounds them. It also includes any special achievements and accomplishments that you can identify.

The purpose of the work history assessment is to find out what jobs you have worked in over your career. You want to look at job titles, industries, dates and reasons for leaving. This will immediately help you to see if you can categorize the industries that you have worked in or if the titles of jobs you held years ago are still valid. Of course, we will also find out that company name changes have occurred and references are no longer available. That's OK. This is simply the documentation section to help you identify problems.

You may be worried as you start this exercise that you have changed jobs frequently or on the other hand, you may be worried that you have only had one job. PLEASE DO NOT WORRY! Remember, the information developed from this assessment is for your eyes only. It will alert you to potential holes in your experience that will be addressed later. It is simply important that you write everything down. Later on, you will use your good judgement to choose the specific information that you want when it comes time to finalize your résumé.

The work history assessment includes a summary of all of the jobs you have held in your career; it also includes reasons for leaving. This is included on your worksheets so that you will have brought the reasons forward into your memory. You will not include it in the résumé. It is helpful because you are reminded of exactly why you left a job. Believe me, you may very well be asked that question in your interview and you must be prepared to answer it. The person that will make the best impression is the one who has a ready made answer for this question rather than the person who has to think of why they left a job right in the middle of the interview. Also, if the reason might bring you difficulty in an interview, you want to prepare for it So, be sure to list the reason for leaving your jobs.

Fill out Your Work History Assessment

Start by filling out the work history list. Continue making a list on your own paper if you run out of room. Remember, you want to develop your work history information as completely as possible but you will only be using part of it in your final résumé. The unused information will be kept on hand for further reference and if required, it will be easy to put into an updated or revised résumé.

Begin with your most recent work position. Try to keep a timeframe of 10 years in mind. Describe all of the jobs over the 10 year period. For any job older than 10 years, you must ask yourself - *does this job add value to your present career direction?* If so, then complete the information.

Example Work History	
POSITION TITLE	Adminstrative Manager
PLACE OF EMPLOYMENT	Calmar Manufacturing
ADDRESS	Anywhere City, USA
DATES OF EMPLOYMENT	2000 – 2008
REASON FOR LEAVING	Laid off (economic-recession)
REFERENCES AVAILABLE	Yes, favourable, would need forwarding address of supervisor

Format Your Work History Summary

Now that you have completed your work history assessment, you are ready to transfer this information to the résumé. For the purposes of your draft résumé, use a separate sheet of paper for each résumé section. Once completed, keep it so that you can integrate it into the rest of the résumé.

The transferable résumé style also has another unique feature - it follows the way we read (i.e., from left to right). Therefore, wherever possible, critical information is put on the left so that we see it first and it stands out. List the titles of your job on the left, then the name of your company, with the dates. Use capital letters and bold print as shown in the

Your Work History Assessment

Please feel free to copy extra pages as you need them.

Position title	
Place of employment	
Address	
Dates of employment	
Reason for leaving	
References available	

Notes

Write anything that comes to mind that you might want to look at again. For instance, did you solve any special problems that you could use in the discussion of accomplishments? Write a few notes here just to jog your memory.

example. When you have completed the entire résumé, you must go back and decide what type of font is best to use. It doesn't matter, as long as it has a pleasing visual effect on the reader.

Formatted Work History

ADMINISTRATOR, Finance Department, McLeod Construction, 2004 - present

ACCOUNTING CLERK, Finance Department, Mars Plastics, 1999 – 2004

Remember: you are the product!

The most common mistake people make when they format their résumé, is to highlight the name of their former company in **bold CAPITAL LETTERS**. Ask yourself, who are you trying to sell with your résumé? Your former company or yourself? Place your job title in bold, not your former employer.

Formatting Tips

Every person is unique and has their own unique set of circumstances that are sometimes hard to translate into a résumé. The following tips will help you get over some of these rough spots.

- If you have always lived and worked in one location, then to restate this location; i.e., Anywhere City, USA, is redundant and boring. Eliminate the location all together.
- If you are still in your current job, you can use the word *present* instead of a date.
- We often find that our job title changes over time but that the actual duties do not. If this is the case, put the current job title, but include all the other titles in brackets so that you can easily refer to them. Then, when you finalize the résumé, decide which title to use. Use only one title; the preference is for the current title.
- If the job responsibilities changed as well as the title, you may well decide to state this as another job. Do so if you believe that it is distinct enough. It does not matter at this stage because you will be selective in your final draft of the résumé.

There are times when your job title is so specialized that it does not mean very much in the general market. If this is the case, you should look for a parallel title that you might possibly use. Put this title in brackets near your original title. You can decide which one to use at a later time.

One problem that often arises is the dates and months of the year that you began or ended a job. A good approach to that problem is this:

- If the job is six months or less, then include the months; if the job is more than six months then use only the year. For example: January - April 1981 (less than six months).

Summer employment and part-time employment can be a problem when trying to describe this work on a résumé. For instance, if you worked at the same summer job for three summers, you could write the description like this:

SURVEYOR ASSISTANT, Bowman Construction, 2000 - 2004, Summer Employment

If you held the same kind of job but with different companies you could state the industry rather than a specific company.

TRADES HELPER, Construction Industry, 2004 - 2008

The same problem can arise for those who have had full time, regular part-time jobs or casual positions for a time. In this situation, put the titles all on one line. Example:

HEALTH CARE AIDE, Dysan Centre Hospital, 2001 - 2008, Regular, part-time, casual

In some cases, people act in a more senior position on a temporary basis. These acting positions are usually of short duration but the employee can take an acting position several times during one working year or within the career time frame. It is difficult to advise on this problem in a general sense but there are a few ways that this can be handled. If you have had a number of acting positions that represent a promotion over the years of your employment, you can isolate this as a 'new" job. For instance, a lead-hand in a manufacturing plant who was acting in the foreman position for periods of three to six months at a time over several years, may be able to state this higher level of employment in this manner:

ACTING FOREMAN, CNC Manufacturing, Anywhere City, USA, January - October 2007

- If you have been out of work for some time, you have to find some way to explain what you have been doing. If you have been doing contract or consulting work then use the terms contractor or consultant.

CONSULTANT/INDEPENDENT CONTRACTOR, Lincoln Manufacturing, 2004 - present

02. Your preferred work environment

You have now completed your work history assessment and you have confirmed where you worked and what jobs you have worked in. Now is the time to ask yourself – what did I like (or not like) about each work environment? Review the notes section of your work history documents to see if you jotted down any information that can be helpful here.

Jot a few answers to the following questions in the note spaces provided. Confirm with yourself:

What did you like about working at each job?

Would you want to work in that kind of work environment again?

03. Education / Professional Development

Now it is time to look at your qualifications in the areas of formal education or professional development. Once again, for the purpose of the draft résumé, use a clean sheet of paper for this section. The rough draft will list all your formal education and your professional development. When this is done, decide what order to put it and where in the résumé to insert it.

Organizing and Prioritizing

Once you have listed your formal education and/or professional development qualifications, ask the following questions to help you prioritize your list.

- What kind of eduction do you have? Is there more formal education than informal professional development?
- What is more current, your formal education or professional development? Depending on the number of courses/programs/certificates, try putting the most current formal education first.
- What sells you the best – your formal education or your professional development? Choose whatever sells you the best and list this first.
- Where did you take your formal education, in your country of residence or another country? Is your education recognized or reputable? You will want to include your education but displaying your professional development first may sell you the best.
- Review your list for visual effectiveness. Use bold or italic fonts or create two lists separated by a space. Move these résumé pieces around until you are satisfied that it gives you a strong position statement about the qualifiations you offer and is visually appealing.

Formatting Your Education And Professional Development

As you will see from the following example, there are three sections – formal degrees, formal certificates and professional development. As well, you should use the full name of your university. If it causes the date to run on the second line, then try to use the abbreviations as shown below.

Although the professional development in this example is more current, the sample candidate felt that the academic degrees were more important. In this case, it was also felt that there was additional credibility given by adding who sponsored the professional development courses. Depending on the number of courses, this may be optional because it tends to make the résumé look visually crowded.

EDUCATION

MASTER OF EDUCATION, Personnel & Administration, U of M, 2000

BACHELOR OF EDUCATION, Secondary Studies, U of W, 1995

BACHELOR OF SCIENCE, U of W, 1994

Certificate, *Administrative Leadership*

Certificate, *Special Education*

Certificate, *School Psychology*

Managing Conflict in Today's Schools, Dept. of Education, 2001
TQM in an Educational Environment, M.T.S., 2000
Developing Positive Work & Home Relations, Department of Education, 2000

If you have a long list of professional development workshops, then review the list and select only the most current (i.e., last 5 years) or make your selection based on any other appropriate criteria. The résumé must be visually balanced as well, so if your list simply looks too long, reduce the size of the list.

There will be times when you feel the professional development is not only more current but also more relevant than a degree. In that case, put professional development as the lead set of statements.

Formatting Tips

Once again, every person will have a unique problem when it comes to trying to state education and professional development qualifications. The following tips may be helpful but it must be emphasized again– What adds value? What sells you the best? Only you can decide.

- You can make the decision on whether to include dates or not. If the topic is more influential than the date, then exclude the date.
- If including dates makes one or two of your courses look too outdated, then don't use dates at all or use only current dates for the first three or so of your list.
- If you do not have a degree or certificate, then leave education out and use only the title Professional Development.
- If you only have one or two courses and they are somewhat outdated, then leave the section on professional development out of the résumé.
- If you have neither an education or professional development that would add a positive tone to the résumé, then leave the whole section out. Of course, you'll have to make up for this with all of your work accomplishments!

04. Community/Professional Leadership

The next section of the résumé will help show your initiative and leadership accomplishments in either your community or in your profession. It includes all volunteer work, whether it is for your church, volunteer in a seniors home, for your community club or for a professional association.

Write your community/professional leadership jobs in the same manner as you did with your paid jobs. Make copies of the worksheet provided for you.

Formatting Your Community/Professional Leadership

In this example, the candidate chose to separate the professional volunteer service from the community service, because the employer to whom they were applying would more greatly appreciate the professional leadership. Depending on the length of the lists, you might also choose to use bold capital letters or lowercase bold italics. Sometimes you have had several leadership positions with one organization; if you have three or less, list them as in the example below, if you have more, then you will have to carefully assess the visual effects of repeating the one organization too many times.

COMMUNITY/PROFESSIONAL LEADERSHIP

Chairperson, Saskatchewan Society of Engineering Technologists

Treasurer, Saskatchewan Society of Engineering Technologists

Member, Saskatchewan Society of Engineering Technologists

Club Leader, Boyko Community College

President, Mystery Readers Association

Parent Volunteer, Readview Day Care Centre

Reminder: Rewrite your Community/Professional Leadership qualifcations on a separate sheet of paper. Save it to integrate with the rest of your résumé.

Your Community/Professional Leadership

Please feel free to copy extra pages as you need them.

POSITION TITLE

NAME OF ORGANIZATION:

DATES:

RESPONSIBILITIES:

SPECIAL PROBLEMS/PROJECTS:

Notes

What did you like about this work environment?

Job Title/Position	What did I do?	How did I do it?	What skills did I use?
Manager	corporate budgets treasury financial planning	consolidated 7 divisions strategic planning project leadership	communication solid financial skills coordination
Volunteer Coordinator	organized annual banquet	called parents and asked for volunteers and donations selected time, location got notices ready made arrangements for entertainment	interpersonal communication coordination planning scheduling
Computer Systems Administrator	provided technical support and maintenance services ensured data integrity and long term storage	responded to calls on a timely basis learned the design of the company systems participated in the setting of policies and procedures	technical proficiency in hardware platforms and a large variety of software applications ability to learn new technologies quickly skilled in translating and simplifying technical concepts to end users good detail orientation and project management skills
Receptionist	received incoming mail received phone calls confidential correspondence	date stamped, sorted, prioritized screened calls, took messages keyboarding/Word computer skills confidentiality communication	organizational skills customer service tact and diplomacy
Homemaker	raised three kids worked on farm led volunteer women's group	developed and managed three personalities read parenting books cooking, canning, gardening budgeting tutoring/homework running meetings	communication humour create own pattern follow detailed pattern creativity following directions managing a budget organizing coordinating problem solving
High School Grad— School Studies	studied seven subjects wrote essays, exams, did projects	developed a study schedule and followed it located and did research on topics used the computer	organization and coordination skills self-discipline, time management responsibility writing, editing skills research and analysis ability to work independently and on a team

Formatting Tips

- Once you make your list, decide if you have more community versus professional leadership. This will decide which title to put first. If you only want to use one title, that's fine. You can use bold caps, similar to your job sheets or bold italics or plain italics. Try out different fonts – remember, visual impression is important.
- If you do not have any volunteer experiences, then leave this section out. If you only have one or two statements for this section, you will have to decide if they add any value to your résumé.

You have now completed three sections of the résumé; work history, education/professional development and volunteer/professional leadership. The arrangement of the various sections of your résumé will depend on what sells you the best. There is no one right answer! Leave it until you have finished your skills analysis but do a first pass look and ask yourself what order would sell you the best?

These sections were the easy part of your résumé. Now you will move to the hard part – that of identifying your skills.

Assessing Yourself

05. Identifying Your Professional Expertise/Skills

Most of us tend to think about our duties, in other words, what tasks we did in our various work placements. For the transferable skills résumé, you must think about how you carried out your tasks and what skills your tasks required. It is these skills and the sum of all the skills that you have acquired over your lifetime that will help you find another job.

So, it is important to look carefully at every job or volunteer leadership position no matter how long ago. You need to look at all of your tasks no matter how trivial they appear. You need to identify all the skills you have developed whether they were gained through paid or unpaid work. Let's begin.

Use An Assessment Framework

Make a copy of the worksheet provided to help you to answer the three key questions stated below.

The key to the skills based résumé is to ask yourself:

1. **what did I do?**
2. **how did I do it?**
3. **what skills were required?**

Fill out these worksheets for every job and volunteer position that you have had. Keep going until you have exhausted all of your ideas or at least until you start to see a pattern developing. Only then will you be ready to classify and categorize these skills.

A number of examples have been done for you, demonstrating that this assessment tool can easily be used in any paid or non-paid work situation. Then, you will see a blank worksheet for your own use. Make yourself several copies.

When you are doing your skills assessment, keep going until you start to feel you are repeating yourself. This will mean that you can start seeing patterns in your skill sets. Once you get to the point of considerable repetition, then you know you are finished.

Categorize Your Skills

You have now completed a skills worksheet for each paid job and/or your volunteer activities or leadership roles and you have seen skills repetition or patterns emerge.

Next, you need to classify and categorize your skills. Use the Skill Cluster Chart to group your skill sets. Look them over carefully. What do you see? Write all of the patterns down in the worksheet. To begin, simply create your summary list. Then ask yourself – can I categorize some of my skills? Once you have finished that task, you need to name your skills....are they communication skills? Management/leadership skills?

Your Skills Assessment

Please feel free to copy extra pages as you need them.

Job — title/position
Company/Organization Name

What did I do?	How did I do it?	What skills did I use?

Review the following example.

PROFESSIONAL EXPERTISE/KEY SKILLS

- technical skills – finance
- treasury
- accounting
- planning, organizing and coordinating
- supervising
- leadership
- analyzing, synthesizing
- teamwork

Your next step is to list and prioritize your skills in the order that best markets you. Number them or rewrite them from highest priority (the skills you want to use in your next job) to the lowest priority (a skill you can do but don't particularly like and don't really want to do a lot of in your next job).

Build Your Expertise Statements

Through this skills assessment process you will have identified specific skills, clustered them together and prioritized them. Now is the time to create your expertise statements. These skill statements will be set out in the résumé in the following manner. Note that the heading will be either Professional Expertise or Key Skills – whatever you feel comfortable with.

PROFESSIONAL EXPERTISE/KEY SKILLS

- Priority #1 Skill Statement
- Priority #2 Skill Statement
- Priority #3 Skill Statement
- Priority #4 Skill Statement
- Priority #5 Skill Statement

Skill Cluster Chart

Please feel free to copy extra pages as you need them.

Name of Skill Cluster	Name of Skill Cluster	Name of Skill Cluster

Tips For Building Expertise Statements

Note: Do not overflow to the second page unless it is absolutely necessary.

- Choose the heading that you are comfortable with, either *professional expertise* or *key skills.*
- Include no more than approximately seven to ten statements in your résumé. If you have more than ten statements try to reduce the overall list.
- Be careful with the descriptors (i.e., extensive, excellent, superior or good). Make sure that you can defend the mastery level that you say you have. Do not be repetitive.
- Skill statements are often hard to write, therefore the beauty of this book is that the skill statements are done for you. You simply refer to a skill, read the list of skill statements and select the one that best suits you or, use the example and write your own. Transfer this to your draft skills page.
- Make any other special changes that you want. These statements are simply frameworks from which to build your own statements. It is rare that you can use exactly what is written. You must make them your own. After all, you will have to defend them in an interview.

Barbara J. Bowes
48 Résumé Drive, Winnipeg, Manitoba, R0X 3B6
Phone: 1-809-224-9993 Email: you@youraddress.com

Highly skilled manager of diverse organizational functions. Strategic planner who takes initiative and is innovative, creative, and meets goals. A leader who is a trainer, facilitator and team builder. Bottom line manager who increases productivity and organizational effectiveness. Highly organized with good communication and interpersonal skills.

Professional Expertise

- Priority #1 Skill Statement
- Priority #2 Skill Statement
- Priority #3 Skill Statement
- Priority #4 Skill Statement
- Priority #5 Skill Statement

The résumé skill statements always start with a word that describes the strength of your skill. Use words such as significant, excellent, or well developed. The statement should describe the skills you have. Sometimes you can add a component that demonstrates what you can do with that skill. We have listed a sampling of skill statements for you.

SAMPLE PROFESSIONAL EXPERTISE STATEMENT

- Excellent strategic organizational planning and coordination skills for project and program initiation, staffing, start up, implementation and timely completion with limited budgets and resources.
- Good supervisory strengths for staff management, delegation, supervision, training and conflict resolution.
- Good interpersonal and leadership skills for facilitation of a positive team-oriented management style in both corporate and regional work environments.
- Corporate level financial and economic analysis skills complemented by experience in major acquisition, divestiture or capital expenditure decisions.
- Extensive and successful experience and expertise in financial resource acquisitions and management, equipment procurement and budget development.

Putting it Together

06. Building Your Personal Profile

The next important part of the résumé is your summary profile. It is situated at the top of the résumé and is a synopsis of the skills you offer. The summary profile should not be written until you have confirmed all your skills. **Please note that we do not label it as summary or profile.**

To help build your Personal Profile, you can also refer to the sample list of fully developed profiles.

THREE KEY THINGS ARE INCLUDED IN THE SUMMARY

- Who you are (personal style traits).
- What key skills you have.
- What are you looking for in a job match (This can sometimes be omitted).

The descriptors that are recommended in the summary are those that reinforce what the reader will see described under the key skills or professional expertise section. ***The idea is that in a 10 second glance – the reader can see who you are, what key skills you have and what you are looking for in your next job.*** This section usually requires a great deal of writing and rewriting. Don't be discouraged. Start broadly and keep working the words until they are as clear and succinct as they can be. This 10 second glance will cause the reader to set your résumé aside to read in greater depth at a later time and you'll stay on the "A" pile of résumés.

Typically, the summary is highlighted by using bold or bold italics, to help catch the readers eye. Read the following example.

PERSONAL PROFILE

Results-oriented generalist with versatile experience in administrative and human resource management, staff recruitment, selection and training. Strong interpersonal and communication skills. Well developed analytical, creative problem solving, and decision making capabilities. Easily adaptable to change with a willingness to learn new concepts and technology. Demonstrated ability to work both autonomously and as a team player. Built long term relationships of trust and respect.

07. Identifying Your Accomplishments/ Achievements

You have now completed page one of your résumé. The next step to building your résumé is to examine your accomplishments or achievements. These are then incorporated into page two of the résumé.

What are accomplishments? What are achievements? People are always confused about this. We seem to believe that the only achievements that count are the achievements of acquiring $1 million or saving your company $1 million. This is not true! Let's look at what an achievement or accomplishment really is.

An achievement and an accomplishment are the same thing. It is a task that you completed or carried out successfully, or a task that you finished to your satisfaction. It is a problem that you solved that had a noticeable result or improvement. The problem can be simple or complex.

When identifying problems or projects to use in the accomplishment section, list a large number of problems and then select one that demonstrates the largest number of your skills. Try to keep the accomplishment list to a summary of three major problems that best cover all your skills. This makes it easier when you are in the interview as you can refer to the same problem or accomplishment more than once by expanding on certain components of the problems.

Using an Accomplishment Achievement Assessment Framework

The best way to find out and be certain that you identify your accomplishments is to take a problem solving approach. It works this way:

- Go back and look at a job duty or task.
- Ask yourself – what problem(s), challenges or barriers did I face in carrying out this responsibility? List them.
- How did I solve this problem? What did I do? (List at least three)
- How well did my solution work? What was the result?
- Write up an accomplishment statement. Write the statement by incorporating the answers to the above question.

Copy the worksheet provided for you.

Job Duty/Task	Problem
• organize a fund-raising event	lack of volunteers
	Solution
	• went to local school and offered a reference to those students who helped in our campaign
	Positive Result
	a successful fund-raiser

Accomplishment Statement
Overcame a lack of volunteers by offering senior high school students exchange for a reference resulting in a successful fund-raising campaign of over $100,000.

SAMPLE ACCOMPLISHMENTS

Acted as a facilitator at conferences and designed and/or delivered training courses on such diverse subjects as sexual harassment, telephone systems, effects of technology on the work place, interview techniques and assertiveness training.

Communicated effectively and diplomatically with professional colleagues and subordinates as an analyst and a director, as an intermediary for the executive, and as an advisor to boards and senior political officials.

Developed strategic and operational plans, policies and procedures for the leadership and management of an organizational unit consisting of 40 departments, a staff complement of 535 and an enrollment of 4,000 full-time and 19,000 continuing education students.

Enhanced institutional profile and recognition by ensuring the increase of accredited programs. Provided executive support for the achievement of national or provincial accreditation of 16 programs over a seven year time period.

Established emergency policies and procedures for fire protection, electrical, fuel and vital services including fire fighting procedures, plans of action, coordination of plans, salvage procedures and contingency plans.

Reviewed and critiqued strategic plans for numerous Crown corporations operating in the utility, government services, and commercial sectors including integrating the major facilities planning process for a large utility working with the President and a task force of representatives of the key functional areas.

Your Accomplishments/Achievement Chart

Please feel free to copy extra pages as you need them.

Job Duty/Task

Solution

Positive Result

Accomplishment Statement

Interview Strategy

One of the reasons the skills or competency based résumé is so effective is that it closely parallels the behavioural descriptive interview approach that is now so popular with employers. Behavioural descriptive interview questions ask for real live situations of where you solved a problem or successfully overcame a challenge. Behavioural questions will start like this, *"tell me about a time when.....you were most challenged, most proud...."*

Or they may refer to a specific work related situation and ask, *"tell me about a time when you successfully overcame resistance about a new idea..."*

So how does this new behavioural interview style relate to your résumé? First of all, the way in which you identify your accomplishments fits exactly with the way in which the behavioural questions are asked. So, by doing your résumé this way, you are far ahead of the game.

The challenge however, is that you may be asked to provide additional examples of the same skill. Therefore, I recommend that for every skill you say you have, prepare at least three accomplishment statements. Next, select the most comprehensive one for your final résumé. The most comprehensive accomplishment more than likely includes some of the skills in your other accomplishments. This strategy gives you an advantage because if you are asked for another example in an interview, you can easily provide it as you are already well prepared. Believe me, there is nothing more embarrassing than answering one question well and then stumbling on the second question because you can't think of a good example on the spot.

Read the following sample accomplishment statements. Once you have written a few accomplishments and you understand the framework, then you may feel confident to let go of the chart and simply write the accomplishment freehand.

08. Finalizing Your Résumé

Page One is Critical

Now is the time to put all of the résumé pieces together. Remember page one is always the same – the personal profile and professional expertise. It looks like the example below.

Barbara J. Bowes
48 Résumé Drive, Winnipeg, Manitoba, R0X 3B6
Phone: 1-809-224-9993 Email: you@youraddress.com

Seasoned human resource professional with senior leadership experience during a time of significant change and rapid growth. Demonstrated expertise in managing organizational change and integrating HR services to different business models within an international environment. Seeking a new challenge to contribute at the executive level.

Professional Expertise

- Skilled at providing overall strategic leadership to an HR department delivering the full spectrum of HR services including employee relations', collective bargaining and collective agreement administration; health benefits services, compensation, recruitment, occupational health and safety as well as supporting the delivery of all HR practices and policies.
- Well developed strengths in championing corporate human capital strategies and the development of best practices through a Business Partner relationship to senior executives.
- Senior level skills, expertise and experience in workforce planning and ensuring the alignment of the people and business strategy across the corporation.
- Keen ability to create and apply metrics and key performance indicators to confirm the contributions of HR to the business goals.
- Experienced in the oversight and maintenance of the HRIS, quality control and protection of employee data.
- Skilled in the design and implementation of all human resources policies and procedures associated with all HR initiatives to ensure alignment with corporate objectives and risk management.
- Strengths in the effective management of all talent management, organizational development, training and development, and succession planning initiatives.
- Strong proponent of diversity in employment; strengths in developing excellent working relationships with various ethnic employment agencies.

Tips for Selecting and Ordering Key Résumé Components

- Page one – the statement of skills is compulsory. All other pages of your résumé are flexible and are dependent on what section sells you the best. Here are some tips to help you decide.
- Page arrangements can also be different depending on the length of information provided. You need to be careful with your list as it may appear overwhelming. A safe approach is to have one half of the page as accomplishments and the remainder displaying one or two other categories. It is important that you "play" with this to see what structure gives you the best visual image.
- If work history is your next best section, then include it on page two if you have room.
- For those individuals fresh out of school, or for those who believe their professional development is their greatest asset, then the education/ professional development section may be best placed on page two.
- For those individuals who are considered re-entry, your accomplishments in the voluntary sector might be appropriate or you may decide to display your volunteer leadership.
- The arrangement of all other sectors following section one are your choice. Simply make sure you put your best features first.

SAMPLE ACCOMPLISHMENTS

- Accomplishments 1
- Accomplishments 2
- Accomplishments 3

PROFESSIONAL LEADERSHIP

- Leadership 1
- Leadership 2
- Leadership 3

WORK HISTORY

- Employment 1
- Employment 2
- Employment 2

The Finished Resume

You have now finished your resume. Remember, the only compulsory page format is page one. After that, it is you who decides what to place where. Keep in mind the question – What sells you the best?

Select the font and style that gives your resume the best presence. Change from bold capital letters to italics or whatever will give you a good visual presentation.

Two complete sample resumes have been included for you. Although names and places are fictional, these resumes have been created by real individuals. Several additional examples are provided at the end of the book.

Barbara J. Bowes
48 Résumé Drive, Winnipeg, Manitoba, R0X 3B6
Phone: 1-809-224-9993 Email: you@youraddress.com

Human resource generalist with over three years experience in a fast paced manufacturing work environment. Excellent planning and organizational skills for the effective implementation of new programs and initiatives. Good training skills and experience, able to take responsibility for new employee orientation and exit interviewing. Seeking additional responsibility and new learning opportunities in the HR role.

Professional Expertise

- Solid academic background in human resources accompanied by additional inhouse training programs in effective report writing, conflict resolution and team building.
- Well developed human resource generalist skills with experience in new employee orientation, front line supervisory training and performance evaluation.
- Skilled in planning, preparing, interviewing potential candidates and preparing recommendations for line managers; good experience in reference checking and preparing onboarding materials.
- Clear understanding of the impact of absenteeism; developing effective consulting skills in early return to work and employee accommodation programming.
- Growing expertise in the management of employee benefits accompanied by participation in salary surveys and job evaluation.
- Results oriented professional who thrives on taking on and learning new tasks; willingly provides support to HR manager and front line supervisors.
- Developing leadership skill with experience in leading small specialized project teams to design and recommend program changes.
- Detail oriented with well developed writing skills; able to effectively participate in policy development and the writing of employee handbooks and training materials.

Accomplishments

- Led a team of 4 HR professionals to conduct focus groups of front line supervisors to evaluate the effectiveness of the corporate performance management system. Project resulted in numerous recommendations which were presented to HR management.
- Met with representatives of workers compensation board and followed their advice to make recommended changes to the early return to work program; was recognized by management as "employee of the month."
- Over a seven month time frame, reviewed the internal HR policy manual and identified several areas requiring revision; was assigned the task to revise and ensure policies were compliant with legislation.
- Participated in and became one of three professionals certified in an inhouse, "Results Centred Leadership" program.

Community/Professional Leadership

Member, Society for Human Resource Management

Member, Arlington Toastmasters Club

Volunteer, United Way Grand Forks

Education

PHR Candidate, Human Resource Certification Institute (HRCI)

B.Comm (HR major), American Intercontinental University

Certificate, Dale Carnegie Public speaking

Work History

HR Generalist, BusinessPro Software International

HR Generalist, City of Grand Forks, one year term

Student intern, City of Grand Forks, three months

Barbara J. Bowes
48 Résumé Drive, Winnipeg, Manitoba, R0X 3B6
Phone: 1-809-224-9993 Email: you@youraddress.com

An accomplished personnel/administrative professional with over twelve (12) years extensive experience in public sector, manufacturing and service industries. Detail oriented with commitment to high standards. Seeking professional challenges and career opportunities to become a key contributor in a team-oriented environment.

Professional Expertise

- Efficient personnel and administrative management skills specializing in recruitment, selection and placement of professional and non-professional employees to meet the company's and clients' manpower requirements at the lowest possible cost.
- Solid background and thorough experience in the formulation and implementation of personnel policies, psychological testing, performance evaluation, wage and salary administration and computerized payroll using the Royal Bank system.
- Effective counselor in handling confidential personal and work related situations or problems of employees, clients and applicants.
- Excellent people skills and in depth sensitivity to the needs of individuals at all levels with openness, directness and fairness.
- Proficiency in prioritizing workloads, up-to-date personnel data bank and complete detailed documentation of interview/counseling reports.
- Successful track record in determining, developing and delivering tailored to fit, in-house seminar packages.
- Well developed interpersonal and communication skills; able to relate to a variety of people within the work setting.
- Strong detail orientation; familiar with HRIS systems, able to oversee data input and ensure accuracy and updates.
- Good understanding of compensation and benefits; able to assist in annual salary surveys and compensation updates.

Accomplishments

- Over a four year timeframe, worked as a placement consultant. Successfully placed over 500 employees in a variety of industries at a cost effective rate.
- In an emergency situation, acted as a peer mentor to a suicidal employee; was able to prevent personal harm and get help.
- Recognized as employee of the year for ability to provide excellent customer service on behalf of the human resource department.

Work History

Personnel consultant/counsellor, *Donna's Personnel Services* May 2005 – April 2008

Personnel/payroll Manager, *Sports club pant/Canadian menswear* Feb. 2004 – April 2005

Personnel/administrative manager, Donna's collosol career centre
Jan. 2000 – Jan. 2004

Education/Professional Development

Business Management Forum Federal Business Development Bank July 19 – August 27, 2008

Career Assessment Instruments for Business Industries, 2004

Labour – Management Cooperation for Industrial Peace & Harmony, 2004

Time Management, 2002

HRD in Focus/Bridging the Effort for Survival, 2002

Alternative Management Style, 2000

Personnel Management, 1996

Expertise Statements

The following section contains skill statements that you can choose to use for your own résumé. You can use the statements exactly as they are or make minor changes and make them your own. Note: these expertise statements are listed alphabetically.

Accounting/Financing

- Accuracy and consistency complemented by excellent skills for the completion of bookkeeping and accounting tasks, journal entries, coding invoices, compiling data, preparing financial summaries, posing and balancing.
- Bottom-line financial orientation with creative leadership in resource allocation enabling a balanced budget and ongoing monitoring for eight divisions comprised of 40 departments with 80 full time and 36 part-time programs.
- Corporate level financial and economic analysis skills and experience in major acquisition, divestiture or capital expenditure decisions.
- Demonstrated bottom-line accomplishments through solid supervision and management of financial reporting and control functions in a multi-million dollar operating environment.
- Excellent auditing skills, both external and internal, for the examination of records to disclose areas of loss under tax legislation or company policy procedure.
- Excellent treasury and banking expertise including negotiating and structuring corporate credit facilities, foreign exchange and interest rate risk management, cash flow management and related policy development.
- Highly skilled in the design, revision, implementation and maintenance of accounting reporting systems for management and shareholders in sophisticated computerized environments.
- Keen business acumen and expertise in strategic financial planning resulting in business development, growth in profitability, and sales and overall financial success of an organization.
- Strong accounting skills with extensive experience in sourcing and implementing manual and computerized accounting systems to process monthly financial statements, general ledger, accounts receivable, accounts payable, payroll and year end financial statements.

Administrative Support

- Ability to adapt generic systems to meet specific company needs by compiling, planning and writing office material manuals for future use.
- Highly developed administration strengths for the establishment of effective policies and procedures for general office management.
- Mature with discretion and judgment in handling confidential information.
- Strong ability to focus on policies and procedures, and development and control in corporate administration, operational, finance, treasury, and human resource areas.
- Well-developed organization, planning and administration strengths for confidential, corporate level services in sensitive executive and ministerial work environments.
- Skilled in the development and preparation of confidential correspondence, reports and policy manuals.
- Detail-oriented, skilled and experienced in coordinating and confirming schedules and deterring appointment conflicts.
- Efficient administrative and organizational abilities; skilled at word-processing, management, assembly of monthly reports, and researching and making travel arrangements.
- Proficient in the operation of a busy switchboard and reception area, able to communicate with callers in a professional and customer service manner.
- Highly developed organizational, administrative and financial management strengths utilizing continuous quality improvement for the efficient and effective management of office structure, day-to-day operations including systematizing allocation of resources and monitoring workload.

Analytical/Problem Solving

- Creative problem solving approach to meeting customer needs complimented by a keen ability to initiate, recommend and create strategic alliances with interested key stakeholders.
- Demonstrated analytical, innovative and creative problem solving and decision making capabilities coupled with effective trouble shooting skills developed through productivity analysis of measurable results.
- Excellent problem solving and conflict resolution skills for participatory staff involvement and issues management.
- Excellent analytical strengths for complex organizational analysis, productivity improvement, work simplification, job analysis and major systems design.
- Highly developed analytical skills supported by demonstrated strengths in financial management and computer business applications.
- Innovative problem solver; able to proactively develop efficient solutions to challenges in a variety of work environments.
- Keen problem solving strengths with an innovative, creative approach to resolving problems and challenges.
- People-oriented, humanistic approach to problem solving with keen ability to develop trust in an encouraging and supportive work and customer service environment.
- Solid foundation and significant expertise in the application of process improvement and total quality strategies in all areas of operations management in order to ensure the highest standards of customer service.
- Visionary strategic planner with keen ability to identify and assess the impact of changing environmental conditions on an organization, match resources to short and long term goals and set priorities.

Business Development/Planning

- Accomplished ability in business plan development and achievement of revenue and profit.
- A keen profit awareness not only for initiating client programs which protect company profits and produce volume but also by preparing and managing department budgets effectively with a constant examination of creative cost savings.
- Demonstrated ability to manage over 200 clients maintaining accurate record administration and ensuring prompt collection of accounts.
- Demonstrated bottom-line accomplishments attained through solid supervision and management of operations in a multi-million dollar operating climate.
- Entrepreneurial and innovative, with an attitude towards success, complemented by intense results-oriented drive.
- Exceptionally creative with substantial ability and success in the identification of customer and business trends, the identification and exploitation of market opportunities, conducting competitive analysis and the initiation and design of co-venture programming.
- Keen business development skills for evaluation, goal setting, start-up opportunities, acquisitions and joint ventures with successful bottom line performance.
- Proven resourcefulness and innovativeness in startup, day-to-day operations and damage control within the oil, mining, aerospace and hi-tech manufacturing sectors.
- Proven track record in developing existing business and identifying and pursuing opportunities.
- Solid business acumen with extensive experience and educational foundation in business start-up, management, promotion, marketing and sales.

Communications/Public Relations

- Assertive and effective communication skills; able to provide written and verbal summaries/briefings/reports that are easily understood and logically presented.
- Assertive and effective communication skills when interacting with the public, committees, board of directors, community organizations and government agencies.
- Effective communication skills for the establishment and development of strong working relationships with business, industry, education and government colleagues as well as staff at all levels.
- Excellent communication and interpersonal skills for effective teamwork, staff management and the development of sound working relationships with suppliers, clients and customers.
- Experienced in the research, development, implementation and evaluation of communication strategies.
- Good communication and interpersonal skills complemented by strong organization and ability to work both autonomously and as a team player.
- Quietly assertive with excellent communication skills enabling a solid relationship with suppliers, bankers, lawyers and auditors.
- Significant oral communication and presentation skills for direct sales solicitation, sales presentations, and internal staff training and development.
- Well developed communication skills for effective customer/staff relations.
- Well developed research and interview expertise combined with strong presentation skills.
- Working knowledge of radio and television production as well as limited experience with on air responsibilities.
- Significant creativity for concept and implementation of unique and effective public relations and marketing strategies in multi-task, change oriented and time sensitive environments.
- Excellent strategic organizational planning and coordination skills for projects, events and program initiation, staffing, start-up implementation and timely completion within limited budgets and resources.

Community Development

- Able to analyze and prepare detailed feasibility studies and develop an implementation framework and action plan for community and economic development projects.
- Able to administer an economic development fund and conduct post loan counselling and project evaluation.
- Highly skilled in the directing and coordinating of input required for economic development projects from project description through to monitoring.
- Strong understanding of and ability to promote programs and services to targeted clientele.
- Superior level of expertise and knowledge of community resources and support networks for education, self-improvement and family assistance which enables effective service for children and families.
- Thorough understanding of program design, development, implementation and evaluation of new or existing initiatives.
- Solid working knowledge of community collaboration concepts for the development of action projects directed towards the improvement of quality of life.
- Highly skilled in the application of strategies and mechanisms to link ad hoc community initiatives and groups into established structures.
- Well developed community development toolkit, inclusive of techniques, discussion and decision making techniques, action planning tools, process review strategies, and evaluation tools.
- Highly skilled at quickly understanding the context of a community, gaining a basic knowledge of the community and its dynamics including the community's history and culture, changing economic base and demographics.
- Strengths in the conduct of a community situational analysis inclusive of the community social and decision making power structure and processes.

Computer/Information Technology

- Able to install and upgrade server application tools, allocate systems storage, plan for future storage requirements, create primary database storage structures, modify database structures and provide security services.
- Ability to plan and implement information technology strategies, and develop user teams for large scale technology transitions.
- Broad knowledge and experience in matching appropriate technologies, designs and systems development techniques with organizations needs, capabilities and resources.
- Computer literate in both mainframe and personal computing utilizing spreadsheets, word processing and automated office, including local and wide area networks.
- Documentation expertise in the areas of forms design, screen design, user guide development, application guide development, document cataloguing and management, workflow analysis and DIP experience.
- Excellent skills in software development including the design, enhancement, and maintenance of existing software products.
- Highly skilled in using a structured development methodology approach, data modelling, systems documentation and project management information.
- Strong computer expertise for major computer program revisions, planning, research, trouble shooting, and consultation within an office environment.
- Strong knowledge of business software and hardware. Hands on understanding of selection, implementation and operation of systems to achieve cost effectiveness and strategic advantage.

Customer Service

- Expertise in customer service and the resolution of customer dissatisfaction.
- Good customer service orientation for working with a wide range of clientele including the disabled, senior population, children, public and private sectors.
- High degree of professional integrity with excellent public relations strengths resulting in the development of solid business relationships with customers and suppliers.
- Proven customer service focus complemented by administrative management strengths to build work systems that support consistently high service standards.
- Solid communication and interpersonal skills for good working relationships with customers; able to assist from identification of needs to completion of tasks.
- Solid foundation and team membership experience in developing a total quality management and innovative customer service corporate culture.
- Strong sense of customer service with experience in the field of service and sales.
- Superior customer service focus with keen ability to develop and exceed service excellence in a total quality service environment.
- Well developed customer service philosophy with proven skills in the development of award-winning service standards.
- Solid customer service philosophy with a focus on customer satisfaction and the development of long term relationships with customer and suppliers.
- Well developed active listening skills; listens without interrupting while effectively clarifying and verifying information.
- Maintains a professional approach and presents a positive image to internal and external people when representing self, service and the agency.

Counselling/Employee Assistance

- Able to act as counsellor to subordinates and peers on matters related to career advancement, abuse, harassment and other personal matters that may have impact on an employee's job performance.
- Cool head in a time of crisis with expertise in the prevention of suicide.
- Empathetic listener with intuitive strengths and rapid decision making ability.
- Strong assessment skills for the identification of client's physical, emotional and spiritual need prior to placement of appropriate personnel.
- Superior empathy, interpersonal and communication skills with ability to foster personal growth and empower client contacts.
- Well developed interviewing, counselling and analytical skills, able to quickly understand and identify client needs and issues; establish safety and security and facilitate effective problem resolution.
- Holistic counselling and conceptual framework, skilled at identifying client needs and systematically integrating selected methods and approaches to facilitate client behaviour change.
- Well developed socio-emotional skills; able to respond spontaneously and effectively to a wide range of client needs, able to assist clients in both one-on-one and group intervention strategies.
- Highly skilled in the application of cognitive learning and restructuring approach, able to challenge self-defeating client beliefs and attitudes and assist clients to mobilize resources towards building personal independence.
- Well developed interviewing, counselling, mediation and analytical skills; able to be understanding while quickly identifying client needs and issues, establishes client comfort and security, facilitates effective programs of problem resolution.

Government/Regulated Environments

- Experienced in the participation of government advisory committees and coalitions in the areas of government restructuring, race relations, diversity, discrimination, and equality and community development.
- Highly developed political savvy and judgement skills for working with elected officials, boards, agencies and the public, complemented by extensive experience in negotiating multi level collaborations and strategic partnerships.
- Highly skilled in consultation and collaboration with government and community agencies to spear-head, design and develop policies and programs to promote multiracial harmony.
- Highly skilled in the leadership of task forces and committee structures which require collaboration with unions and community stakeholders to design, develop and strategize the application of new and broad ranging policies and programs.
- In-depth working knowledge of board-managed associations, combined with good group facilitation skills for project management and community leadership.
- Keen understanding of and practical management experience in a highly regulated environment with a working knowledge of municipal and provincial legislation regarding mineral claims, land rights, general leases, railroad leases, as well as health, safety and environmental regulations.
- Keen understanding of municipal and provincial government functions with the ability to write, present, defend proposals, and work collaboratively in sensitive and dynamic relationships.
- Significant expertise and experience in the proactive development of policy initiatives in the areas of culture and race relations within municipal, provincial, national and international environments.
- Well developed understanding of government structure and processes with ability to lead, manage and chair various committees and task forces which provide for public participation into facilitating legislative change.

Hospitality

- Detail oriented with well developed skills in the analysis of administrative, financial and inventory systems, policies and procedures. Proven strengths in the design, development and implementation of organizational structures to support retail and hospitality environments.
- Excellent coordination and organizational skills with successful accomplishments in large, high profile culinary events, professional and political conferences.
- Good understanding and ability to monitor market trends, create and develop new catering menus, catering manuals and develop and deliver customer service training programs.
- Proven ability to manage complex events and projects to successful completion in large facilities of up to 35,000 square feet of conference meeting space.
- Proven strengths in financial management including budgets, cost based analysis, point of sale and inventory control systems and marketing plans within the hospitality industry.
- Public relations strengths and interpersonal skills for effective development of business and working relationships with customers and suppliers.
- Solid foundation in hospitality systems with keen ability to identify problems and increase productivity and profitability through staff recruitment, selection, training and continuous improvement programs.
- Solid organizational skills for the successful operation of a 220 seat, full service restaurant with consistently high achievement ratings for service, cleanliness, procedural integrity and guest service as determined by a corporate testing division.
- Superior customer service focus with keen ability to develop and exceed service excellence in food and beverage operations for hotel/resort environments.
- Well developed abilities to lead and participate in the design and development of multi-million dollar expansions of guest rooms, food and beverage facilities including equipment procurement.

Human Resources

- Accomplished human resource management strengths including compensation, staffing, interviewing, performance reviews, job descriptions and evaluations, conflict resolution, training and teambuilding.
- Demonstrated ability to integrate human resources with other corporate business plans to attain productivity improvements and cost reductions.
- Excellent interpersonal and human resource management strengths with capacity to work with a variety of people in a dynamic, supportive and participative work environment.
- Expert knowledge of benefit designs, contacts, underwriting, pricing, administration, claims control and accounting.
- Proficient in utilizing innovative ways to recruit, motivate and develop a work team environment within a non-profit environment.
- Solid expertise in the design and development of human resource compensation and benefit systems including flexible benefits, cost containment, early retirement and pension planning.
- Solid human resource management skills including planning, recruitment, selection, supervision, employee relations, salary and benefits administration, contract negotiations, training and development, personnel policy development, job descriptions, performance appraisal and job evaluation.
- Solid human resource, team leadership and interpersonal strengths for the motivation and management of professional, technical and administrative staff components.
- Solid understanding of employee benefit programs with specific skills in the research, planning, analysis and negotiation of the most cost effective plans.
- Solid working knowledge of current legislation regarding labour standards, fair employment practices, collective agreements, health and safety and unemployment insurance with ability to undertake responsibility to ensure company compliance.

Information Technology

- Extensive experience in automating the process of software development: creating scripts for generating code for database objects, Delphi and Java classes, etc.
- Very strong coding and debugging skills, can easily understand code written by others.
- Extensive experience as a Solutions Architect at the enterprise level in designing systems and solutions to meet the business need of the organization; demonstrated expertise in database design, development and tuning with all database technologies.
- Solid background in web-based application design and development, user-experience design, operational support and project management at the enterprise level.
- Ten years experience designing Oracle-based solutions for large high technology corporations. Technical and functional proficiency with the Oracle Applications suite of products.
- Experienced at selecting and managing technology vendors and professional services organizations as well as presenting IT issues and solutions to senior management teams.
- Practical experience with the following technologies:

  Java/J2EE, Visual Basic, Perl, XML, C/C++, Python, HTML, JavaScript, Adobe Flex,UML Modelling.

  Vignette Portal and V7 CMS, Stellent CMS, Fatwire CMS.

  Oracle CoreID, Sun One LDAP.

  Oracle DB, mySQL, PostgreSQL, Apache and Zope.

  Solaris, Windows NT/2000/XP, Linux.
- More than 15 years of experience leading all stages of SDLC. This included requirements definition, analysis, architecture, design, implementation, testing, risk management, deployment and support.
- Designed, developed and implemented solutions for Enterprise Architecture including Business Architecture, Data Architecture, Applications Architecture and IT Architecture.
- Etions, data/project archives and disk maintenance.

Interpersonal Skills

- Effective interpersonal skills in multi-disciplinary and team environments for efficient utilization of all resources.
- Excellent interpersonal skills resulting in above standard staff performance and reduced absenteeism.
- Excellent interpersonal skills resulting in the establishment of terrific working relationships with all internal, external and government advisors.
- Excellent interpersonal communication strengths with a flair for group dynamics and the development of solid relationships and networks.
- Good interpersonal and leadership skills facilitating a positive team-oriented management style in both corporate and regional work environments.
- Solid interpersonal skills with demonstrated ability to direct individuals in a team concept environment which includes fellow workers, clients and the general public.
- Superior interpersonal skills for the interpretation of corporate and employee needs, allowing for the provision of relevant, timely and accurate information dissemination.
- Well developed interpersonal skills ensuring effective dealings at all levels of an organization.
- Solid interpersonal and human resource management strengths with the capacity to work with a variety of people in a dynamic, supportive and participative work environment.
- Demonstrated experience in human resources management complemented by well developed interpersonal skills and a proven track record in the establishment of positive working relations with all levels of personnel.
- Strong interpersonal and communication strengths; able to quickly gain trust with people at all levels of an organization.

Leadership

- Effective leadership and team building strengths; able to analyse requirements, identify skills and motivate a team to successfully complete projects.
- Effective supervisory strengths for the management of a multi-unit organization with varied levels of professional and administrative personnel.
- Effective task orientation with expertise in delegating responsibility, ensuring harmony, establishing work priorities and schedules, dealing with concerns of clients and staff, conducting reviews and evaluations of systems and programs.
- Management team leadership strengths with specific expertise in delegation of responsibility, establishing commitment, setting work priorities and schedules, addressing concerns of customers and staff members.
- Natural leadership strengths with strong communication and interpersonal skills for effective development of sound teamwork relationships.
- Participative team management style with a strong focus on identification of staff roles and responsibilities; articulation of clear, concise and accurate expectations; and the provision of employee development.
- Practical, hands-on approach to problems with solid technical ability to manage small financial and construction problems.
- Proactive team leadership skills; capable of innovative and practical problem resolution in the financial, administrative and staff development areas.
- Quiet, mentor/leader management style with ability and experience in supervision of technical personnel in a laboratory and machine shop environment.
- Strong leadership, communication and consulting skills for executive management, directorship and committee chair in the private sector, not-for-profit sector, and service organizations.

Negotiation

- Conciliatory expertise utilized in developing and maintaining satisfactory relationships within a unionized environment.
- Creative expertise in negotiations preparation, strategy and tactics.
- Effective and persuasive negotiation strengths with a deep appreciation of the quality and value of a diverse group of people holding wide ranging views.
- Effective and persuasive strengths with demonstrated use of the win/win processes to gain consensus and understanding.
- High level of expertise in complex negotiations for union/work agreements, compliance to regulatory control legislation and land/lease agreements.
- Keen intuition and the ability to counsel, negotiate and resolve conflict.
- Negotiation strengths with ability to negotiate contracts with vendors and external clients.
- Proven investigative and negotiation skills ensuring effective and appropriate intervention.
- Solid working knowledge of contract negotiations and capital acquisition with ability to review and input to a variety of contracts and legal documents.
- Strengths in the negotiation of agreements with a customer driven environment.
- Strong belief in win/win negotiation processes for agreement and understanding.
- Superior negotiation skills for the achievement of cost savings, profit targets, and profits.
- Strong interpersonal and negotiation skills, effective communication to all levels including senior managers, government, volunteer boards and executive, consignors and colleagues. Equally strong in oral and written modes of communication.

Conflict Management

- Strong understanding of conflicts as an organizational process; skilled and experienced in the design of policies and processes that constructively draw conflict to the forefront and provide opportunities to resolve issues effectively.
- Holistic approach to effective conflict management, exceptional understanding of organizational dynamics; supportive of participatory processes to developing high quality dispute resolution.
- Well-developed systems thinking approach to organizational changes and conflict management; able to assess interrelated areas of dysfunction and develop collaborative strategies for intervention.
- Experienced in participating in a corporate alternative dispute process; trained in joint problem solving methods, able to act as a neutral advisor.
- Well developed understanding of the methods, principles and stages of systems design for conflict resolution; experienced in facilitating group conflict sessions.
- Confident in personal conflict resolution skills, keen sensitivity and strengths in the identification of special issues, able to clarify and prioritize issues for resolution.
- Developing strengths in conflict management; able to facilitate front line group conflict sessions resulting in consensus decision making and resolution.
- Is able to be objective in the identification of situations needing attention; is able to step in and de-escalate conflict.
- Highly skilled at masterfully defusing challenging conflicts; willingly steps up to conflicts and provides unbiased intervention.
- Employs optimal timing for making a decision to employ alternative methods of dispute resolution. Maintains effective control over processes and focuses on desired outcomes.

Non-profit Management

- Experienced in not-for-profit organizations including the incorporation, establishment of policies and procedures of volunteers and fundraising.
- Highly skilled in the recruitment, training and coordinating of volunteers developing volunteer recognition programs.
- Significant expertise and experience in the role of Executive Director, with strengths in administrative operations, supervision of staff, preparation and presentation of financial reports, program and policy development, implementation and administration.
- Significant strengths in board management at the local, provincial and national levels.
- Skilled program development specialist with ability to initiate, design, develop, implement and evaluate both small and large scale programs.
- Well developed skills in working effectively with volunteer boards and committees to prepare intermediate operational and business plans.
- Skilled at building and sharing a compelling view of the direction of the organization; is able to engage and motivate others toward a common goal.
- Excellent strengths and ability to work cohesively with key association stakeholders including board directors, members, political appointees and community groups and the administration. Able to acknowledge the diverse needs of all interested parties.
- Demonstrates a long-term strategic focus; is able to balance short and long term goals and objectives while managing the day-to-day implications of board strategy.
- Skilled in developing budgets for strategic resource plans and communicating them to administrative and professional staff.

Operations Management

- Able to manage all responsibilities of print shop operation including tendering, quotes, stock ordering, artwork delegation, printing job, collating, cutting, folding and final packaging, account preparation, postage metering, mail handling, inventory and stock control as well as budget preparation.
- Ability to initiate and manage office administration including receivable and payable accounts, correspondence and record keeping.
- Accomplished at developing management systems and effecting change through skill development and coaching.
- Competent administrative skills with ability to undertake budgeting, analyze variance and profitability reports.
- Consistent and successful record of managing financial budget and operational resources in a wide range of administrative positions.
- Detail-oriented with well developed skills in analysis of administrative, financial, and inventory systems, policies and procedures.
- Proven strengths in the design, development and implementation of organizational structures to support corporate environment.
- Executive level management and team leadership skills for tackling the full range of executive concerns and issues.
- Excellent operational and administrative expertise for the functional management of a corporate branch office.
- Excellent strategic strengths with keen ability to develop operational plans to meet organizational goals.
- Extensive, in-depth, executive management skills and experience in large, multi-service, multi-project, retail sales environments including travel and entertainment.
- Extensive experience and expertise in strategic and operational planning with skills in the management of planning with a large and complex work environment.

Organizational Skills

- Adept at managing details with ability to plan, schedule, analyse needs and develop priorities in order to carry out responsibilities in an independent manner.
- Excellent organizational abilities with extensive experience in the public sector, municipal committee leadership as well as small business start-up and management.
- Excellent organizational and administrative ability with superior strengths in planning and attention to detail.
- Excellent organizational and planning strengths for large facility and events management including policy development and implementation, formulation and implementation of business plans.
- Excellent organizational skills for the accomplishment of tasks within a specific timeframe.
- Excellent organizational skills for delivery and prioritizing service in a client sensitive environment.
- Excellent organizational skills with ability to manage a large residential facility including staff supervisors and maintenance and customer relations.
- Good organization and planning skills for policy development, formulation and implementation of a formal business plan, including forecasting, budgeting, and attention to the bottom line.
- Organizational strengths for planning, scheduling, implementing and follow-up of varied, multi-scoped projects.
- Proven ability to organize single and multi-unit operations resulting in increased sales and customer satisfaction.
- Skilled in managing details with ability to plan and schedule, analyze needs and priorities and carry out responsibilities in an independent manner.

Policy Development/Analysis

- Able to supply meaningful input for the development of corporate policy.
- Proficient in the communication of results to members, customers and company personnel.
- Extensive experience in policy analysis and development in formulating corporate/department goals and in providing leadership to achieve target results.
- Highly skilled and extensive experience in the development and implementation of policy manuals which include job descriptions, employee orientation and performance evaluation programs.
- Skilled in the creation of policy, procedure and administrative manuals, able to maintain significant numbers of confidential client records.
- Skilled in the interpretation of the impact of local and national policies.
- Skilled in the systematic collection, analysis and presentation of data for the evaluation of programs and policy effectiveness.
- Well-developed field work techniques for policy and program review, strengths in research design, sampling procedures and measuring outcomes.
- Skilled in the conduct of operational reviews for evaluation of program compliance and policy implementation.
- Experienced in program review and evaluation in the areas of education, social welfare, health, housing, mental health, legal services and economic development.
- Solid working knowledge of and experience in effective planning and policy analysis; skilled at researching contingencies and alternatives for policy implementation.

Project Management

- Action-oriented, innovative, able to meet time and budget targets by strategic planning while employing logic and ingenuity.
- Excellent abilities to follow instructions and to complete responsibilities within assigned deadlines.
- Extensive experience in initiating and coordinating complex corporate projects.
- Excellent project management strengths for successful and timely completion of complex work programs within contract framework.
- Excellent strategic organizational planning and coordination skills for project and program initiation, staffing, start up, implementation and timely completion within limited budgets and resources.
- Good project management skills with ability to cost estimate, identify and allocate resources, and follow work through to completion and provide appropriate evaluations.
- Significant working knowledge of business process re-design with experience in arranging cost control inventory systems to limit stationary retention.
- Solid project management skills complemented by high quality work standards enabling the completion of work within difficult time frames.
- Strong organizational skills for developing and implementing complex projects with a keen awareness for deadlines.
- Superior project management skills with significant expertise in the management of diverse projects including identification of issues, planning, implementation, and monitoring for successful completion.
- Excels at identifying, scoping and planning comprehensive and complex projects; skilled at writing a high level scope of work including justification, product description, major deliverables, success criteria, high-level time and cost estimates, assumptions, and constraints.

Research

- Able to conduct data collection for acceptance test reports, component failure analysis and trend analysis; able to test and troubleshoot computers, printed circuit boards, power supplies, cables and components.
- Excellent investigative skills and ability to develop conceptual frames and theories using the principles of irreversible thermodynamics.
- Highly sophisticated strengths in atomic physics, fundamental quantum theories, applied mathematics, non-linear analysis and physical chemistry.
- Significant laboratory skills for the preparation, organization, and coordination of test experiments involving interdisciplinary teams of physicists, chemist and engineers.
- Significant numerical methods research strengths for studies in radiative transfer in the atmosphere, gas ignition and biomass systems, and fluid flow.
- Significant research skills for assessment, feasibility studies, preliminary design, and evaluation studies within the environmental engineering studies field.
- Solid working knowledge of scientific investigation of biophysical and biochemical processes using the principles of irreversible thermodynamics.
- Strengths in managing a multi-disciplinary scientific and technological research project, complemented by extensive experience in negotiating multi-partner collaboration.
- Well developed ability to conceptualize, research, organize and implement specific projects.
- Well developed research and writing skills with experience in writing and editing a weekly economic analysis report outlining the agricultural conditions.
- Well developed research and writing skills complemented by the ability to translate scientific technical documents between English, French and German.

Sales and Marketing

- Accomplished at creating marketable and profitable products and services.
- Dynamic, creative sales and marketing techniques enabling the attainment of corporate team objectives.
- Exemplary knowledge and application of the psychological principles of selling, complemented by very strong interpersonal skills which confirms abilities as a team leader, trainer and coach.
- Extensive and diverse experience gained through effective experience within the major retail trades ranging from the sales floor to the board room to successfully implement corporate selling plans.
- Highly skilled in idea generation and promotional planning. Able to create and implement plans including special events, direct sales, sales incentive programs, price lists/catalogues and shows to achieve and exceed sales objectives.
- Highly skilled in promotional planning and design including special events, sales promotion packages and annual marketing plans utilizing a variety of mass media.
- Skilled in strategic planning for corporate marketing and sales programming complemented by a strong personal customer services and customer satisfaction philosophy.
- Strong ability to be a calculating risk taker who implements creative, practical solutions for achieving both company and client success resulting in mutual satisfaction and long term relationships.
- Superior skills in the initiation, management and growth with strong emphasis on enhanced corporate image and client relationship building.
- Superior strategic planning strengths in sales and marketing with the unique ability to conceive, design and implement internal and external corporate programs.

Strategic Planning

- Ability to initiate, develop and implement short and long term strategies and their associated tactics.
- Able to participate as a key member of the management team to provide the backup and technical assistance to develop a strategic plan ensuring the growth of an organization.
- Action-oriented innovator able to meet time and budget by strategic planning while employing logic and ingenuity.
- Effective strategic planning strengths with the ability to create a long-term focus and to communicate this information to all levels of the organization resulting in business development and growth in profitability.
- Excellent strategic strengths with keen ability to develop operational plans to meet organizational goals.
- Strategic planning insight complemented by rigorous analytical capability developed through experience with a variety of companies in different situations and industries.
- Substantial skills in strategic planning for the development of long-term corporate plans complemented by ability to focus activities toward the goal.
- Well-developed strategic planning skills to analyze and determine the short term and long term organizational directions.
- Keen sensitivity to organizational dynamics and the impact on strategy implementation; skilled at developing accommodating processes to facilitate internal support for new initiatives.
- Solid understanding of the political strategy and techniques for the development of aggressive competitive strategic action plans; skilled at leading the assessment of business trends, threats and opportunities, internal and external political capabilities and the negotiation of alliance opportunities.

Teamwork

- Ability to gain the confidence and support of employees in respect to integrity and fair play.
- Ability to work both as a team player and autonomously complemented by good communication and interpersonal skills.
- Detailed and results driven with participative management style emphasizing individual growth, active involvement and increased team morale.
- Excellent interpersonal and human resource management strengths with capacity to work with a variety of people in a dynamic, supportive and participative work environment.
- Self-directed, energetic team leadership strengths with a preference for undertaking significant responsibility.
- Solid foundation and team membership experience in developing a total quality management and innovative customer service corporate culture.
- Solid knowledge of group dynamics with keen sensitivity to team members and an ability to form, direct and lead multi-disciplinary professionals.
- Strong organizational strengths for the supervision, coordination and implementation of management work plans, process improvement initiatives and staffing in a fast paced production environment.
- Team-oriented individual with good interpersonal skills for good customer and staff relations.
- Well developed communication and interpersonal skills for effective teamwork and customer/staff relations.
- Willingly participates and contributes positively by sharing information, listening and accepting others' points of view. Is skilled at giving and receiving constructive criticism while maintaining a positive outlook.
- Demonstrates a belief in the team concept; shows flexibility to new approaches and ideas.
- Encourages and involves other team members by soliciting ideas and opinions to help form specific decisions or plans. Values others' input and expertise and is willing to learn from others.

Technical/Manufacturing/Engineering

- Comprehensive strengths and experience in the fabrication of precision aerospace components, research instruments, health care and other complex equipment.
- Demonstrated ability to provide insight into efficiency production resulting in cost savings and more efficient utilization of human resources.
- Exceptional skills and innate ability in the field of mechanical design complemented by over 40 years of creative and practical experience in a research, clinical and prototype environment.
- Good technical skills for the maintenance of small machines such as photocopiers, cameras, VCR's and drill press.
- Highly developed technical knowledge of manufacturing processes, control systems and engineering projects.
- Proven resourcefulness and innovativeness in the start-up, day-to-day operations and damage control for the oil, mining, aerospace and hi-tech manufacturing sectors.
- Solid foundation and working knowledge of machining, manufacturing processes, drafting, CAD drafting, joining technology, welding, surface finishing, mechanical actuators and mechanisms, electro mechanical devices, motor and gear drives, hydraulics, air controls, photography and carpentry.
- Solid maintenance and property management skills for effective facility upkeep, security provisions and equipment control.
- Well developed skill in the utilization of many metals and common plastics particularly as employed in medical applications.
- Extensive experience in the evaluation, selection, installation and commissioning of a wire variety of manufacturing equipment in diverse environments.
- Ten years experience designing Oracle-based solutions for large high technology corporations. Technical and functional proficiency with the Oracle Applications suite of products.

Total Quality Management/Quality Assurance/Business Process Redesign

- Able to lead, guide and train quality inspection work force teams to promote and maintain an acceptable level in quality at the least cost.
- Able to use quality expertise to provide technical assistance to manufacturing departments, investigate and provide feedback on quality problems.
- Advanced quality management expertise including statistical process control, gage record and calibration systems and failure mode and effect analysis.
- Excellent ability to develop quality manual documentation which meets quality audit inspection and national standards.
- Outstanding and thorough application of problem solving and trouble shooting techniques with exceptional enthusiasm towards continuous quality improvements.
- Significant working knowledge of business process re-design with experience in arranging cost control inventory systems to limit stationary retention.
- Skilled in the investigation and feedback of information on quality problems; able to analyze data, initiate corrective action reports and lead meetings to deal with non conformance.
- Skills and experience in the writing and updating of Quality Assurance Operating Procedures, test procedures and manufacturing processes and the development of manuals and instructional tools.
- Skilled quality auditor for FordQ101, including special expertise in failure mode and effect analysis, advance quality planning, statistical process control, gage record and calibration systems.
- Well developed skills and experience in the conduct of quality planning improvements, process capability studies, document preparation and supervision of quality improvement projects.
- Well developed training methodologies for the guidance and training of inspection work teams to promote and maintain acceptable levels of quality for the least cost.

Training and Development/ Group Facilitation

- Ability to facilitate group discussions and planning meetings in order to develop consensus decision making between the varied interests of multiple stakeholders.
- Comprehensive training expertise complemented by extensive people skills, able to provide guidance and leadership resulting in significant employee contributions.
- Demonstrated workshop design, development and delivery strengths with ability to apply skills in a wide range of interesting and challenging environments.
- Highly skilled in the design, development and delivery of presentations in the classroom and on the job.
- Proven training and development consulting skills with specific strengths in board development, problem solving and staff training.
- Skilled in the preparation of training manuals based on government legislation, policies and practices with consideration of the cultural milieu in which the training is taking place.
- Solid foundation in adult training and development skills, expertise and experience in technical training, organizational change and assertiveness leadership.
- Solid success and over six years' experience with disabled client rehabilitation; e.g. job teaching, monitoring progress, evaluating performance and conference reporting.
- Specialized skills in the development of training programs including product knowledge, communications and research.
- Strong foundation in adult learning principles with extensive experience in the design and delivery of staff development programs.
- Strong training skills with proven experience in working with people of all cultures and backgrounds.

Workplace Health and Safety

- Good training skills for the development and delivery of regional training programs in the transportation of dangerous goods, WHMIS and quality customer service.
- Keen political acumen with expertise in the impact assessment of policy, procedures and regulations on health care in particular in the nursing profession.
- Solid knowledge of cleanliness health standards for working in a public working environment.
- Keen political acumen with expertise in the impact assessment of policy, procedures and regulations on health care in particular in the nursing profession.
- Sold understanding of workplace health and safety standards and ability to maintain quality control and represent department issues on Workplace Health & Safety Committee.
- Solid understanding of workplace health and safety requirements; able to provide consultation to managers and training to staff and team leaders.
- Significant expertise and experience in acting as an auditor of occupational health and safety management methods and techniques including hazard identification and risk assessment, selection and implementation of appropriate hazard controls, developing proactive and reactive performance measures, understanding techniques to encourage employee participation and evaluation of work-related accidents and incidents.
- Strengths in evaluating how an organization's activities, raw materials, production methods and equipment, products, byproducts, and business management systems impact occupational health and safety performance in the workplace.
- Highly skilled at identifying and creating work procedures that control risks; skilled at monitoring results and effectively assuring worker adherence.
- Well developed skills in training needs assessments; able to accurately specify the gaps between occupational health and safety competencies required by organization.

Accomplishments

Writing your achivements or accomplishments in the same manner as the framework for behavioural descriptive interviewing creates an advantage. You will now also be ready for the interview!

Accounting/Financial Management

- Analyzed and corrected deficiencies in general ledger accounts, substantially improving the quality of financial management and reducing audit fees by $15,000 in the first year.
- Assumed responsibilities of corporate controller for an extended period. Communicated with divisions, established report requirements and deadlines and issued monthly and quarterly financial statements, budgets and profit plans in a timely manner.
- By undertaking the additional responsibilities for the completion of working papers for year end financial statements, was able to decrease external accounting audit costs.
- Coordinated the financial reporting and management information requirements for six separate companies, comprised of up to twenty divisions, using a manual accounting system.
- Designed, developed, negotiated and implemented an electronic payment system resulting in more efficient payment and improved company receivables.
- Identified and investigated discrepancies in financial accounts resulting in overpayments, short shipments and unbilled revenues.
- Pursuant to the sale of the company to a large multinational, redesigned the management reporting, budgeting and financial statement presentations to comply with the new parent requirements.
- Responsible for $4 million in accounts receivable which were maintained and current. Implemented new procedures resulting in cost and time savings.
- Revitalized six businesses and stabilized their cash flow problems resulting in the retention of over 30 jobs.
- Successfully developed cycling collection methods to reduce delinquent accounts, stimulating corporate cash flow.

Business Process Re-Engineering/ Total Quality Management

- Conducted an organizational assessment, identified operational issues, conceived and implemented a strategic plan for improvements which resulted in increased profitability within one year.
- Developed, implemented and led a Total Quality Management program which greatly improved customer orientation and became the role model for the corporation.
- Developed a quality assurance system, eliminating errors in delivery of supplies.
- In the continuous search for excellence, using cost containment and analytical forte; researched, developed and qualified sources and processes ensuring profitability results in excess of one million dollars.
- Introduced a Total Quality Management program to a manufacturing environment focusing on piece work, resulting in dramatic improvements in inventory usage and long-term customer satisfaction.
- Pioneered a customer satisfaction and quality insurance program including SPC and QFD resulting in expanded sales of $2.5 million.
- Spearheaded and implemented team plans to improve customer satisfaction and product reliability resulting in the achievement of national status recognition.
- Successfully supervised a staff of engineers and technologists in a specialized scientific research environment to achieve unique and measurable production improvements.
- Using strong analytical and interpersonal skills, reorganized a department into teams, improving productivity, reducing unit costs and processing time (30%) resulting in an immediate and continued annual savings.
- Utilizing continuous quality improvement techniques with twelve staff, reduced invoice turnaround which resulted in capturing of discounts and reducing inventory shrinkage.

Computer Systems/Information Technology

- Analyzed system needs and assisted design, development and implementation of customized accounting system to replace an outdated manual system.
- Assisted in identifying, purchasing and implementing new computerized equipment for the milling operation increasing efficiency by an immediate 20%.
- Conducted a feasibility study to determine the cost, benefits and implementation requirements for an integrated logistics support system. Considered hardware, software, facility, staffing and training requirements. Study identified high risks and recommended a no go decision.
- Converted manual supply stockroom accounting to a computer application, reducing inventory investment by 50%, shrinkage to less than 1% and reducing overall stockroom labour hours.
- Created and implemented a computerized territory account planning system that facilitated the tracking, analysis and planning of both the specific geographic market plans and the annual corporate market plan.
- Developed and implemented a computer strategy for a large government department which resulted in the use of computer tendering networked with regional offices. Project was completed on time and under budget.
- Established a computerized schedule reporting system contributing to increased productivity and the improvement of order deadline efficiency by 15%.
- Successfully identified and made recommendations on office automation directions for a major public utility with multiple incompatible computer systems, including opportunities for significant cost savings using office systems on a basis for system re-engineering labour intensive clerical tasks such an overdue accounts notices.
- Successfully managed and installed major computer program revisions requiring intense research, planning, and consultation with key stakeholders at all levels resulting in minimum disruption during the implementation phase.

Customer Service

- Conducted and moderated confidential customer focus group meetings which resulted in the compilations of information regarding client expectations.
- Led and pioneered a customer satisfaction and quality insurance program including QDF, resulting in the expansion of sales by $2.5 million.
- Launched a consumer appreciation department resulting in improved business/community relations.
- Planned and undertook a marketing and personal contact campaign which largely increased customer base through new and returned customers.
- Recognized for customer service orientation, ability to coordinate, meet unique needs, and plan for varied social events, conferences, workshops and seminars.
- Through ability to recognize and act on market opportunities, was able to improve the customer/supplier relationship at a bulk dealership resulting in a significant fuel, lubricant and farm supply increase.

Engineer/Environment/Research Science

- Conceptualized and improved yield by 2% in a large processing plant by introducing concepts to refine the technology.
- Designed an optimal numerical scheme to determine density distribution in rocks by sound travel time tomography.
- Developed environmental impact assessment, reclamation and rehabilitation programs, and managed these through a licensing process.
- Developed accurate and efficient methods to obtain solutions and catastrophic points ignition and bio-mass systems.
- Developed and modified matrix solvers arising in various applications from difference and finite element methods.
- Improved and modified variational methods to solve problems, in control theory and systems.

General Management
Operations Management

- As a senior member of the plant engineering layout team responsible for facility efficiency, was able to improve production capability by 300% over a one year period.
- Conducted an individual store needs assessment and using this information as a base, designed, developed and implemented a model for an appliance stock program resulting in the provision of all western stores with the appropriate, workable product for their trading needs.
- Conducted organizational assessments identifying operational issues and initiatives for improvement resulting in increased efficiency, improved customer service and improved gross sales.
- Developed and implemented revised operational methodologies resulting in productivity improvements up to 100% and individual cost reductions ranging to $1 million.
- Devised, developed and implemented corporate 1, 5 and 15 years operating plans.
- Implemented an audit system to identify incorrect freight rates, recovering substantial dollars and avoiding future overpayment and lost of interest.
- Instrumental in the start-up phase of a new $20 million corporation through establishing and implementing administrative procedures, hiring and training staff, coordinating all travel, negotiation of corporate rates, promoting display facility through effective use of print and electronic media, writing and designing corporate information sheets and brochures as well as establishing an executive level administrative and logistical service to a 21-person Board of Directors.
- Led and managed a national business unit with a multi-million dollar operating budget. Maintained the highest client retention rate in the industry. Continually met or exceeded budgeted profitability.
- Maximized safety by introducing new policies, procedures and equipment resulting in a decreased accident frequency and personnel lost time.

Health Care Management

- As an independent contractor, conducted research on palliative care services resulting in the development of a major report and recommendations.
- As weekend senior nurse for a large national health care agency, supervised staff who conducted over 400 scheduled daily visits in the community.
- Co-authored a "Joint Program Protocol" with a major university. Provided leadership to implement the protocol through the development of joint programs in nursing and child care.
- Developed, designed, tested and applied a community based, health promotion and wellness assessment tool to be used as an initial patient intervention strategy.
- Established a system and procedure for the implementation of workplace health and safety standards.
- For a major university, coordinated a community based practicum program for students in nursing, pharmacy and dental hygiene providing orientation, clinical instruction and follow-up.
- Managed and supervised the provision of patient care in a clinical setting with a total departmental budget of $800,000.
- Over a 20-year period, managed and supervised the nursing staff of 30-bed department in a large city facility.
- Participated in value improvement programs that resulted in the change of healthcare practice and an annual cost saving.
- Successfully collaborated with a national nursing service and a professional association to implement a first of its kind health care program with a primary focus on education.
- Led the coordination and implementation of a health care facility accreditation audit. Set out and monitored the project plan, created online access to policies and documents, and adapted to unexpected auditor requests resulting in a successful audit process and recognition from facility executives.

Hospitality Management

- Successfully operated and managed a two location franchise delicatessen type of restaurant. Developed the business and was responsible for financial accountability, sales, purchasing inventory control, staffing and customer relations.
- Conducted an organizational assessment, identified operational issues and designed a strategic plan for improvements which resulted in increased profitability by $7 million over a one-year timeframe.
- Launched and successfully led multi-million dollar renovations and hotel expansion projects which included food/beverage facilities, beach and public areas, in Australia, Canada and the United Kingdom. Resulted in consistent sales and profit increases.
- Established effective control systems, reduced food/beverage costs, utility and administration costs while increasing efficiency and productivity.
- Streamlined operations, improved employee relations and eliminated waste resulting in increased profitability over a six month time frame.
- Through consistent staff training, motivation and evaluation programs, successfully maintained high standards in a variety of hospitality settings ranging from hotels, resorts, casinos and private clubs.
- Initiated, coordinated and directed very successful and profitable national and international conferences and special events and extended full service hospitality products to as many as 10,000 delegates.
- Demonstrated quick, calm, proactive abilities during a major disaster and rescue operation resulting in recovered sales profits by maintaining extraordinary guest and staff relations.

Human Resources

- Conducted a job analysis of the staff sales position. Based on this, developed an orientation program for all new staff inclusive of administrative procedures, key product knowledge and critical selling points.
- Designed national organizational structure, defined and wrote specific job descriptions, developed and implemented leading industry compensation package. Subsequent staff retention rates became industry standard.
- Developed and implemented policy manuals, which included employee orientation and performance evaluation programs. Resulted in improved morale and a commitment to service excellence.
- Developed an organizational policy manual which included job descriptions, customer sales requirements, credit limits, nature of business transactions, work schedules, dress code, employee skill requirements and training reimbursement program.
- Managed the coordination and implementation of changes to the handling of insurance disability claims. Designed new reporting forms resulting in more efficient processing.
- Managed a 130 person volunteer program which included planning selection, supervision replacement resulting in an overall contribution to the success of the Western Canada Games.
- Applied employer of choice strategies to HR practices resulting in recognition as Employer of Choice for four consecutive years.
- Led a team of 4 HR professionals to conduct focus groups of front line supervisors to evaluate the effectiveness of the corporate performance management system. Project resulted in numerous recommendations which were presented to HR management.
- Met with representatives of workers compensation board and followed their advice to make recommended changes to the early return to work program; was recognized by management as "employee of the month."
- Over a seven month time frame, reviewed the internal HR policy manual and identified several areas requiring revision; was assigned the task to revise and ensure policies were compliant with legislation.

Information Technology

- Senior Architect responsible for the lead role in defining, planning and executing strategic, IT-focused business application development initiatives.
- Managed a staff of 6 IT technologists with duties that included recruiting, workload management, general administration, training and development.
- As Solutions Architect, participated in IT due diligence processes for mergers and acquisitions; role included interviewing the target company's IT staff, auditing and inventorying computer systems including business applications, middleware, and hardware infrastructure.
- Successfully engaged as Solution Architect for many projects which involved working with the business and IT stakeholders to design user experience, create system requirements, conduct architecture design, systems and application design, acceptance test plans, and performance/capacity planning.
- Provided vision and technology guidance to the business and development teams related to portal, content management and identity management on the web.
- Acted as trusted advisor to senior management for strategic planning and short-term tactical issues. Participated in strategic planning and management of an IT program of more than $25M annually.
- Designed and architected the company's web portal and content management solutions. Acted as the Technical Architect, Team Lead and project manager for several IT development projects.
- Awarded the `Presidents Award for Excellence` in 2008 for contribution to employer's corporate wide Architecture Standards.
- As senior developer, managed up to 15 technical resources such as DBA's, system analysts, developers and junior developers.
- Designed and developed communication interface with asynchronous data transmission in interaction with bank accounting system specialists. Implemented this interface in the authorization module using PL/SQL.
- Led the collection of system requirements and designed and developed web-based UI using XML, XHTML, JavaScript and server-side application using Servlets.

Manufacturing

- Acted as a key team member in the construction of a new multi-million dollar high technology facility. Computerization of the production system significantly reduced labour requirements.
- As Plant Supervisor, recorded a 20% annual increase in a 95,000 square foot-aging plant.
- Coordinated the transfer of a manufacturing and industrial support centre to a new location. This included thousands of items of manufacturing tooling for over 120 product line items as well as technical publications and documentation.
- Conducted an assessment of maintenance downtime, developed a human resources plan which required skilled millwrights to maintain equipment. Downtime was reduced substantially within a three year period.
- Designed, developed and implemented an Equipment Condition and Operating Security Audit Sheet to be utilized for evaluating machinery, buildings and equipment and estimating replacement cost.
- Designed and supervised the manufacturing of several pieces of equipment including a cabling machine, vacuum loading equipment, dies and various machine components.
- Established emergency policies and procedures for fire protection, electrical, fuel and vital services including fire fighting procedures, plans of action, coordination of plans, salvage procedures and contingency plans.
- Initiated, coordinated and managed an industrial hygiene program including assessments and remediation programs for noise control, crystalline silica exposure, pulmonary function, WHMIS, asbestos, lead, radiation, hearing, soil, P.C.B.'s and environmental workplace safety.
- Researched, designed, developed and implemented an innovative production process and blending formula to increase product yield and plant efficiency.
- Researched and designed new breakthrough, batch processing tanks with specialized liners to withstand abrasion and corrosion. Resulted in major cost savings as well as meeting future health codes.

Marketing

- Co-created and launched a successful marketing plan that has since been adopted by all national competitor agencies as a key component to major fall product launch programs.
- Coordinated cross promotion informational brochures and programs such as a discount card program which resulted in a substantial increase in consumer response.
- Designed and implemented a strong marketing strategy which within the first year, resulted in a turnaround of a three-year company sales decline.
- Designed, implemented and supervised five domestic and imported product lines while consistently meeting annual company objectives.
- Developed and implemented an effective merchandising and marketing program for two major accounts with a combined retail base of 90 stores.
- Designed, developed and consulted on the implementation of private label programs for several national retail clients.
- Identified market niches for new products and services in the environmental field and developed and implemented a program which surpassed first year target goals.
- Played a role as part of a national senior management committee. Redefined the organizational structure, developed, directed and implemented national operations, annual marketing programs to support $120 million in sales, and national employee incentive and development programs.
- Conceived and executed an integrated marketing program for a regenerated product that increased lead generation by 25% and contributed to revenue by $400,000.
- Designed and launched a dynamic website and an online business that enabled customers to create an inhouse resume databank for potential candidates and new employees.
- Created a regular online customer opinion survey that increased lead generation by 40% and enabled employer to more closely focus on urgent customer needs.

Negotiation

- Formulated a strategy for negotiation of $50 million per year energy supply contract. Analysed significantly complex costing and pricing arrangement and negotiated a savings of $750,000 and capital savings of $4 million.
- Negotiated and administered all contracts pertinent to new office premises, the relocation and operational recovery of a ten-person team. Project was conducted on time and on budget.
- Negotiated and administered all leasing and financing contracts for the purchase of equipment ranging from facsimile machines to heavy equipment, computer systems and aircraft.
- Negotiated the rights to use research data developed for a project fully paid by a client at no extra cost to the company.
- Planned, organized and controlled the negotiation of three divisional distribution systems into a single efficient responsive system.
- Successfully conducted meetings with highly technical and diversified clients to develop an environment of mutual confidence for negotiating and securing multi-million dollar contract sales.
- Initiated and successfully negotiated a strategic alliance with a main supplier resulting in a mutually beneficial arrangement and significant corporate cost reductions.
- Led and negotiated all transitional corporate, financial and organizational aspects of several major business acquisitions.
- Negotiated a significant financial package to provide for business acquisitions of a multi-million dollar corporation.
- Successfully utilized negotiation skills to achieve cost savings, profit realizations and good long term relationships with vendors and external commercial clients.
- Over a three year time frame, led the negotiations for a national professional association to develop a certification process that was applicable across international borders. Project was highly political with numerous stakeholders.

Non-profit Management Government Relations

- As Chairperson of a 37-member federal government committee, for 2.5 years, planned all conferences, seminars and related special events.
- Assumed a major and leading role in a consulting team engaged to provide interim management in a major government services organization in a period of major change.
- Coordinated, administered, monitored and promoted a pilot project for a curb side multi-material waste reduction program answerable to three levels of government and a Board of Directors.
- Communicated effectively and diplomatically with professional colleagues and subordinates as an analyst and a director, as an intermediary for the executive, and as an advisor to boards and senior political officials.
- Coordinated both experienced and inexperienced volunteers in the development of a live stage festival in a series of different venues delivered simultaneously. Involved in the advertising, promotion, ticket sales and scheduling for all events.
- Developed strategic and operational plans, policies and procedures for the leadership and management of an organizational unit consisting of 40 departments, a staff complement of 535 and an enrolment of 4,000 full-time and 19,000 continuing education students.
- Enhanced institutional profile and recognition by ensuring the increase of accredited programs. Provided executive support for the achievement of national accreditation of 16 programs over a seven year time period.
- In the role of Corporate Secretary and Acting Vice President-Finance, developed a budget under severe time and financial constraints, and recommended reorganization to several major areas of a large crown corporation.

Project Management

- Custom designed and project managed the installation of the first wheelchair accessible play structure in the city.
- Designed and coordinated a $200,000 renovation resulting in expanded capabilities and improved sales of 25%.
- Established objectives for project management including planning, VIP services, volunteerism and standards for success.
- Facilitated and coordinated the custom design and construction of the first water play structure for an existing city park wading pool.
- Led and conducted an organizational analysis and restructured the organization, resulting in the reduction of overhead costs by an average of 20% while increasing revenue by 30%.
- Spearheaded and led the planning and implementation of renovation projects and equipment/staff relocation. Ensured effective use of limited space and storage with minimal disruption resulting in prevention of total closure of services and loss of revenue.
- Supervised the progress of seven project teams, ensuring that all tasks were completed on time and management was continuously informed of progress and approved adjustments when necessary.
- Acted as the lead for an internal change management design review team and successfully oversaw the implementation of a new telephone system throughout the corporation.
- Reviewed and redesigned the public relations role in a large association; developed relationships with news media, wrote press releases, hosted various public events and successfully increased the visibility and profile resulting in a significant increase in financial contributions.
- Acted as project leader for the design, development and implementation of a new business unit inclusive of staffing needs, technology requirements, office space, furnishings, marketing requirements and change management communication.
- Over a seven year timeframe, provided leadership and management for $1.2M organization; supervised a staff of 12 FTEs, including two managers, plus a pool of regular and part time contractors.

Policy Development/Management

- Appointed by the corporate President to serve on a task force to develop policies and a five year plan resulting in improved quality of programming.
- As a member of a team, researched changes to the Federal Government Operational Planning Framework. Developed a Funding Analysis worksheet to be completed by grant recipients which assisted in the identification of financial mismanagement.
- Conceptualized, proposed and coordinated the development and delivery of the new national policy which accredits experiential training.
- Developed and implemented a record management policy and trained all staff on procedures enabling a government department to conform with the Freedom of Information Act within the required implementation timeframe.
- Developed, documented and implemented policies in key operational areas such as personnel, investment administration and board relations and protocol.
- Designed and managed a specialized corporations creditors arrangement act reorganization.
- Devised and directed over 100 research studies which analyzed the application and interpretation of numerous national statutes, policies, procedures and practices in areas such as taxation, employment, equity, accreditation, broadcasting and race relations.
- Developed a program evaluation model and supportive policies which were flexible, accountable and involved all program stakeholders. The process and its results have received recognition provincially and nationally.
- Established policies and standards for project management including planning, VIP services, and volunteer workforce.
- Using a participative management style implemented policies and procedures for ensuring excellence and integrity in customer relations and service.

Public Relations/Events Planning

- Created and implemented strategic communication packages including event planning, media relations and collateral materials for public and private enterprises.
- Created, promoted and sold seniors matinees. This required extensive organization, scheduling, advertising, direct sales and the management of transportation issues.
- Developed a newsletter as a means of communicating with and improving retention of employees for an internal department. This served as a key tool to develop departmental and individual recognition, share product knowledge and build a cohesive team.
- Devised and instituted various town hall sessions and scholar-in-residence programs resulting in the attraction of international speakers and presenters and capacity audiences.
- For a provincial government department, coordinated communications activities, managed a resource centre and consistently completed projects within predetermined timeframes and budgets, while meeting stringent standards.
- For diverse client groups, prepared attractively presented public education/communication materials which focused on numerous issues of current concern in a variety of disciplines.
- Launched a successful public relations and fund-raising venture which promoted programs and services resulting in increased commitment and overall financial support.
- Led and successfully coordinated all requirements of a five day international conference hosting delegates from 86 countries.
- Organized and coordinated a four day national conference. Required daily interaction with member agencies, international counterparts and government representatives. Prepared conference budget and funding applications and maintained accounts relating to conference.
- Successfully developed good public relations with community agencies and networks giving acknowledgement and praise for liaison abilities from them.

Retail Sales and Market Management

- As regional manager, supervised and worked in conjunction with store managers to oversee and ensure the efficient functioning of retail stores. Volume sales increased by 50% in twelve months. Successfully maintained customer satisfaction and service.
- Contributed $1.5 million of profit in two combined territories by building and maintaining the highest profit margin within the corporate group while operating in a very aggressive competitive market.
- Created innovative field system tools which saved time, and increased planning and target setting efficiency. This included electronic data equipment and user friendly territory call schedules, field reports, easy professional sales techniques and selling formats.
- Developed and implemented integrated distributor, agent and key account marketing plans, thereby aligning price strategies and mutual marketing efforts, resulting in greatly improved communications.
- Developed an innovative marketing plan which increased sales by 220% over six years, and increased market share by 50% during a time of high competition in an industry dominated by four companies.
- Focused the company's market presence and improved customer service through the implementation of a regional toll-free line, increased regional advertising and the establishment and implementation of single desk ordering.
- Identified a former representative's move to a competitor, performed a successful search for a replacement, re-established direct account contact, developed and tracked intellegence and retained $1.0 million sales in a large provincial territory.
- Transformed departmental operating expenses to become largely proportionate to sales performance, thereby protecting corporate vulnerability in difficult economic times and at the same time contributed more than $250,000 of previous annual expense to bottom line profit through an innovative sales approach.

Social Services Management

- Advocated for children with misunderstood and neglected needs. Investigated and determined relationships between children, patients and social workers.
- Analyzed the social and financial efforts of a public housing rent scale on over 2,000 families in seven communities. Used the results to design, develop and present a revised system which was later accepted and implemented by the communities.
- Developed and implemented the computerized Fine Option and Community Service programs currently used by offenders who are unable to pay their fines.
- In order to deal with the results of service cutbacks to client capacity, designed and implemented a quota list system enabling all agencies to priorize their facility usage.
- Played a key role in resolving personal crises and helping individuals regain control over difficult personal situations.
- Designed, developed and delivered a professional development program on family violence treatment, child sexual abuse assessments and therapeutic interventions for agency staff. Program was recognized and adopted across all agencies in the region.
- Took a leadership role in coordinating support services for persons with mental illness. Prepared briefs and petitions, met with political officials, made public appearances and networked with other social service agencies resulting in the funding of a new, interdisciplinary team to ensure appropriate patient care.
- Over a five year time frame, delivered a comprehensive career management program for individuals with disabilities and mental illness. Provided professional support for job search and ongoing support within the workplace.
- Over a period of three years, participated as a key team member in the devolution of a large social service agency into five agencies that were more community based. Project included workforce planning, change management and the development of new policies and procedures.

Technology/New Ventures

- Participated as a key team member in the technical investigation of recurring compressor stalls for a gas turbine engine. The result was a reduction in the rate of stall occurrence. Investigations were conducted for hydraulic system anomalies and mechanical malfunctions with successful results.
- Founded, owned and operated a dealership for several well known large equipment manufacturers. Developed the business from a corner service station to the areas' largest dealership with the most advanced repair and service facility.
- Co-founded a specialized sheet metal fabrication and heli-arc welding company which following the establishment of a diversified product line. The company grew from three to one hundred employees and sales over $6 million in 10 years.
- Founded and owner/managed a new online business venture which was eventually developed into a three-tier marketing business including retail, wholesale and mail-order.
- Researched and formed a new company which offered communication services between aboriginal and non-aboriginal business, markets and cultures.
- After a twenty-five year career in a large corporation, left to start a new family business venture. Developed the business plan, negotiated financial support, hired and trained 2 employees and launched the business within three months. Business is now celebrating 7th year of business success.
- Successfully put a high tech spin on a low tech business by creating a corporate call coordinating centre which then allowed the company to rapidly do all the booking and dispatch for franchise partners. The result was an increased ability to quickly allow franchise partners to enter into the business and to focus solely on growth.
- Initiated, launched and currently continue to manage a homebased, online personal service website which is now generating $10 million per year.
- Following the death of spouse and owner/operator of a thriving business, took over the helm of the company, acquired a mentor and managed the business for over fifteen years. Recently sold company at multimillion dollar price range.

Training And Development

- Acted as a facilitator at conferences and designed and or delivered training courses on such diverse subjects as sexual harassment, telephone systems, effects of technology on the work place, interview techniques and assertiveness training.
- Conducted and moderated confidential customer focus group meetings. Managed a project in conjunction with the university marketing faculty to develop, distribute and analyze a customer survey to learn more about client expectations.
- Co-designed and delivered three programs over a ten month timeframe, requiring a diverse range of knowledge and skill development objectives. Created trainer and trainee manuals and conducted an evaluation of each program.
- In a variety of subject areas, conceived, developed, wrote and published staff training programs; selected and incorporated complementary audio-visual materials which introduced new concepts, increased program and policy knowledge and resulted in the increase of employee productivity.
- Facilitated workshops at both the provincial and national levels on a variety of subjects ranging from small business management to child care.
- Designed and developed individual and group training sessions about the use of databases in various formats, including CD-ROM and Internet, with consistently positive feedback.
- Pioneered a stand alone work processing instructional package and successfully introduced the program on a national basis.
- Recruited and trained specialized staff on a community supplementary school and youth program.
- Researched, designed and delivered office skills programs in both French and English.

Personal Profiles

The following sample profiles are taken from completed résumés and are categorized for your convenience. Once again, locate the profile that best matches you as you describe yourself — transfer it to your summary profile location and work with it. Change words until the statement really does describe you. Although some of samples are long, our rule is to keep it short! But, an overriding rule is that your résumé is your résumé. We can only advise!

Administrator/Administrative Assistant/Secretary

- A self-motivated, energetic, outgoing individual who has the ability to develop high morale within a team environment. Conscientious and dedicated worker with experience in administrative support services. Bilingual interpersonal communication skills capable of initiating a strong rapport with clients, coworkers and management.
- Bilingual senior administrative professional with ten years of broad spectrum management experience emphasizing an entrepreneurial leadership style. Key strengths are in program design, implementation and evaluation and facilitation of an empowered, total quality environment. Hands-on professional challenged by an organization seeking an assertive, results-oriented leader capable of enhancing and expanding the quality and quality of service delivery.
- Energetic, results-oriented corporate executive assistant with significant leadership, organizational and administrative strengths. Confident strategic thinker and problem solver with excellent communication and interpersonal skills, well suited to a fast pace, time dependent environment. Seeking new organizational management challenges that test my expertise.
- Dependable, well organized, team-oriented employee with excellent organizational skills and ability to follow detailed instructions. Able to work with a wide variety of people and to provide warmth and support as needed. Practical-oriented person seeking new challenges.
- Conscientious, self-directed office administrator and senior accounting clerk with progressively responsible experience. Computer literate with key skills in generating financial statements, reconciliation of monthly statements, preparation of cash flow analysis and management of purchasing and inventory control. Seeking new challenges in an office environment.
- Conscientious, resourceful individual with excellent ability to follow instructions, implement and complete tasks. Good communications and interpersonal skills for effective teamwork. Hard working and competent worker with experience in a variety of environments.

Communications/Public Relations

- A dedicated, hard working and versatile corporate relations professional. Key strengths in project management and the hospitality industry with a strong emphasis on customer development and service. Demonstrated experience in sales and marketing, financial management, and budget planning. A proven leader with excellent team building, communication, and organizational skills who is totally committed to my customers and employees.
- A strongly motivated, experienced and results-oriented communications specialist offering production of print materials from concept through writing and/or editing to finished product for presentation. Excellent organization and coordination strengths complemented by the ability to develop and sustain sound working relationships. Seeking challenging opportunities to bring orderly thought processes and creative talents to written communication projects.
- Creative promotional strategist who excels in establishing new markets. Calculated risk player who explores new alternatives to accomplishing goals. Seasoned hands-on business management specialist with a strong team leadership style enhanced by superior strengths in utilizing experience and resourcefulness in realizing goals. Seeking challenging position that would profitably exploit my talents and energy.
- Enterprising, innovative communications professional with significant organizational talent. Creative, resourceful, independent thinker and problem solver with excellent interpersonal skills and an eye for detail. Extensive experience in a flexible, action-oriented, multi-task environment.
- Highly creative, bilingual communications professional with significant strengths in short and long-term communications. Strong expertise in planning, media writing, public and media relations as well as television production. Strong conceptual thinker with an ability to foresee trends and needs. Able to undertake simultaneous projects and adapt quickly to changing priorities.
- Imaginative, innovative professional with a high degree of expertise in the communications and promotion field. Creative and charismatic in interactions with others coupled with an appreciation for an action-oriented, multi-task employment environment.

Customer Service Management

- An exceptional, results-oriented professional with significant experience and expertise in challenging, fast-paced environments. A high achiever with excellent analytical, communication and business process skills. Seeking managerial responsibilities in a customer-oriented investment services firm.
- Conscientious, customer services-oriented print professional with over ten years of progressively responsible experience in offset printing. Well developed communications skills for the identification of customer needs. Well organized with the ability to complete difficult assignments and work well under the pressure of tight time lines. Seeking new opportunities in the printing field.
- Customer service-oriented, management professional and entrepreneur with strong personal initiative and dedication to rural community development. Extensive experience in venture capital as well as development of strategic business planning, personnel and administrative management. Sensitive team player with well developed skills for interfacing with clients, public and private agencies, government, peers and superiors. Skilled in financial management of large scale account portfolios. Seeking opportunity to utilize unique background and skills.
- Highly experienced customer service management professional possessing a proven track record of developing, achieving and maintaining excellent customer and employee satisfaction while safeguarding and enhancing company interests.
- Highly self-motivated individual who enjoys the challenges of problem solving. A team player, implementing new ideas in business and providing superior customer service. Extensive experience in sales and marketing within the commercial and retail sales environment.
- Seasoned customer service-oriented sales professional. Significant expertise in operational management including marketing, finance and human resources. Seeking a position which will utilize my skills and expertise.

Engineer/Research Scientist

- A highly motivated professional with strengths in research, evaluation, planning and training. Possesses superior analytical and problem solving skills with extensive background in univariate and multivariate statistical analyses. Over sixteen years experience in use of mainframe statistical computer packages. Strengths in planning, organization, and establishing cooperative and productive relationships. Able to work with a team or independently. Looking for a creative and challenging work environment.

- A professional engineer possessing extensive senior management expertise in diverse operating environments. Demonstrated proficiency in the integration of people and resources to maximize productivity and increase production. Seeking challenging career opportunity to utilize unique combination of skills and expertise to make things happen.

- A research and development professional who possesses excellent expertise in several mathematical and physical sciences with significant experience in academic research and a specialization in the application of mathematical methods to industrial problems encompassing in particular, modelling and algorithm development. Additional aptitudes include proficiency in R&D project management and rationalization, budget and proposal preparation, technical liaison complemented by excellent interpersonal, organization and motivational skills.

- Highly motivated, results-oriented Engineering Professional with demonstrated expertise in Just-In-Time, Total Quality Management and ISO-9000 standards and their implications in the areas of operational analysis, cost reduction, productivity and quality. Seeking professional challenges which enable significant contribution to corporate goals.

- Multilingual, highly motivated and collaborative scientist who likes to work within a multi-disciplinary environment. Skilled teacher with the ability to develop conceptual frameworks and theories, apply theories to indoor air quality problems, develop concise yet high quality technical reports, and translate documents into French, German and Russian.

Executive Management

- A management executive with expertise in marketing, communications, and program design and delivery. Highly motivated and innovative with excellent organization, supervisory and presentation skills. A demonstrated ability to address issues and achieve results.
- A senior executive with extensive experience in construction product sales, promotion and dealer support work. Technically-oriented professional, with proven success in new product introduction.
- A Senior General Manager with extensive experience in managing operations, finances and personnel with the commercial and retail sales environment. Demonstrated expertise in hiring, training, motivating and terminating staff, market identification and sales projections, general budget preparation and overall financial management to ensure the best possible bottom line results.
- An accomplished executive with excellent communications skills, and proven ability in problem solving, team building, motivational training, client service, and sales management.
- Creative, flexible and articulate senior executive. Possesses demonstrated analytical and organizational skills. Well developed and proven management and consulting expertise in the area of business analysis, TQM, strategic, financial, and market planning, Able to work with a team or independently. Enjoys an environment of creativity and challenge.
- Extensive and diverse background in senior management positions within the hospitality industry. Very effective in maintaining or exceeding profits relative to budget projections, without compromising customer service or satisfaction. Committed to teamwork and development of a sense of professional pride and self-worth within the hospitality and service industry.
- Extensive and diverse background in senior management positions involving marketing, administration, operations, public relations and human resources. Able to develop and maintain budget projections without compromising service or customer satisfaction. A results-oriented professional committed to personal and organizational success.

Financial Management

- Accomplished, energetic financial manager with an excellent combination of formal education and practical hands-on expertise in business management and accounting. Highly motivated, hard working and committed to quality, integrity and profitability.
- Conscientious, reliable individual with a good working knowledge of basic accounting principles complemented by a solid customer service perspective. Mature and responsible work orientation approach to problem solving, with the ability to take the initiative and lead small projects. Seeking opportunities that integrate university studies and previous work experience.
- Experienced financial professional with expertise in analyzing, developing and implementing computer systems. Proficient hands-on developer of spreadsheet and Dbase applications. Team leader committed to developing and motivating staff to meet deadlines on time and within budget.
- Highly motivated, results-oriented, take charge professional with key leadership strengths in organizational development, communications, and financial management. Extensive entrepreneurial, strategic planning and leadership experience in business start-up management and community development. Seeking a challenging career opportunity to utilize my unique combination of skills and expertise in a fast paced working environment.
- Pragmatic, seasoned executive with a solid background and progressive experience complemented by strong strategic planning, organization and negotiation skills. Excellent leadership and general management strengths, with a recognized track record of success in supervising and leading management staff in the attainment of business targets. Seeking a key role in a challenging new environment.
- Results-oriented professional manager/leader. Experienced in all aspects of business and not-for-profit association management. Hands on manager who develops effective subordinates within a team management style. Skilled in operations administration, leadership, communication, marketing, financial management, human resources, planning, corporate reorganization, client service, and government relations.

General Business

- Exceptional leader with proven strengths in communication, team building, interpersonal skills and pro-active customer relationships. Comprehensive experience in administration, budget control, human resources, operations and strategic planning. Professional manager seeking challenging opportunities to contribute to efficient work practices.
- Hands-on, value driven, team leader and astute problem solver, possessing superior financial, communication and interpersonal skills. Achievement-oriented supportive manager seeking new organizational challenges that test and augment management expertise.
- Highly motivated professional with a proven track record as a strategic planner, motivator and team builder. An innovative and creative leader with excellent interpersonal, communication and management skills. A visionary with a keen ability to identify and assess changing conditions in an organization, and match resources to short and long term priorities.
- Highly self-motivated individual who enjoys the challenges of problem solving. A team player, implementing new ideas in business and providing superior customer service. Extensive experience in sales and marketing within the commercial and retail sales environment.
- Independent, self-reliant individual with good business abilities complemented by a keen commitment to customer satisfaction. Eager to be fully active and seeking new employment challenges.
- Keen, responsible, and diligent individual with many years of work experience in a variety of environments. Strong organizational skills with a systematic approach to accomplishing tasks. Strong customer service orientation. Seeking new challenges.
- Professional business leader with key strengths in financial management, strategic planning, organizational development, computerization projects. Possesses an extensive background which includes significant accomplishments in housing, education and child care with a cross-cultural, broad-based governance environment.
- Visionary, diplomatic professional with proven administrative and financial skills, good abilities in oral and written communication; insightful problem solver; effective leader.

Health Care Management

- Experienced, professional manager specializing in the health/service sector. Committed to integrity; pursuing a vision focusing on solutions and turning complex problems into opportunities. Strong analytical problem solving, negotiation and decision making skills with extensive Canadian and International experience in Health and Rehabilitation. Seeking highly responsible management challenges.
- Highly skilled, results-oriented health care generalist with experience in diverse organizational functions encompassing human, material and financial accountability. Able to undertake leadership roles utilizing demonstrated analytical problem solving skills. Well organized with good communication and interpersonal skills. Seeking an opportunity to contribute as a team player.
- Well-organized and effective health care management professional with key strengths in crisis intervention, assessment, planning, implementation and evaluation. Extensive leadership skills in a multi-disciplinary environment. Seeking challenging opportunity to use skills and expertise.
- Results-oriented visionary health care professional with extensive expertise in the critical analysis of issues, strategic planning and administrative management. Conscientious team leader with strong continuous quality improvement perspective. Seeking new challenges in health care.
- Seasoned health care executive with extensive experience in the leadership and management of not-for-profit health care agencies. Well developed strengths in strategic planning, human resource management and board relationships. Seeking new challenges and opportunity to contribute to success.
- Senior facility leader with experience in the leadership and management of multi-site health care facilities. Skilled at leading a team of technical support personnel. Seeking new opportunities.

Hospitality Management

- Highly self-motivated manager with extensive background in the service industry. Demonstrated expertise in exceeding budgeted profit performance while providing superior customer service. Excels in taking on new challenges with proven skills in recruiting, training, motivating staff, overall financial management and general administration.

- Highly self-motivated professional with extensive and diverse background in management positions within the service industry. Demonstrated expertise in promoting, marketing, hiring, training, and motivating staff; budget preparation; and overall financial management to insure the best possible result. Enjoys the challenge of problem solving, being a team leader, implementing new ideas and providing a superior customer service.

- Hospitality professional with key skills in operational assessment, financial analysis and personnel management. Committed to the highest quality of customer service complemented by comprehensive food and beverage experience. Seeking career opportunities to challenge skills and expertise.

- Multilingual, highly self-motivated, hands-on General Manager, with a diverse and international background in executive, and hospitality management. Demonstrated experience in exceeding budgeted profit performance while providing superior customer service. Committed to teamwork and professional pride. Seeking challenging career opportunity to utilize unique combination of skills and expertise in a fast paced working environment.

- Multilingual hospitality professional with extensive expertise in food and beverage management complemented by solid foundation in European professional training. Excellent customer service orientation and ability to plan, coordinate unique social events, conferences, workshops and seminars. Seeking challenging career opportunity to utilize skills and expertise.

- Multilingual European trained hospitality professional with extensive management of food and beverage operations. Total customer service management philosophy complemented by solid organizational abilities and proven skills in financial management, recruitment and motivating staff. Seeking challenging career opportunity to utilize skills and abilities.

Human Resources Management

- An accomplished personnel administrative professional with extensive experience in public sector, manufacturing and service industries. Detail-oriented with a commitment to high standards. Seeking professional challenges and career opportunities to become a key contributor in a team oriented environment.
- A highly motivated, seasoned professional with negotiation and motivational abilities, who enjoys a challenging result-oriented position. Proficient in human resources management including motivation, evaluation, training and supervision. Strong analytical skills in a demanding decision making setting.
- A highly motivated manager with superior analytical skills gained through above average organization and determination. Strong interpersonal, negotiation and communication skills. Well developed problem solving and decision making capabilities. Proficient in human resource management and delivery of quality customer service. A professional willing to learn new concepts and techniques, demonstrated ability to perform accurate work in pressure situations.
- Dynamic professional with proven experience in the field of human resources including training and development. Well developed abilities to plan, organize, and implement successful completion of small business starts, business related projects, and fund-raising events. Independent, motivated and results-oriented with excellent follow-through capabilities.
- Employee Benefits Specialist, able to independently analyze and resolve out of the ordinary and unexpected problems acting with cleverness and timeliness. Confident thinker with facilitative, communicative, interpersonal and presentation skills developed in an employee benefits environment. Able negotiator sensitive to the needs of internal and external customers.
- Human Resource Generalist, with over three years experience in a fast paced environment. Excellent planning and organizational skills for the effective implementation of new programs and initiatives. Good training skills and experience, able to take responsibility for new employee orientation and exit interviewing. Seeking additional responsibility and new learning opportunities in the HR role

Information Technology

- Experienced professional IT Solutions Architect with 20 years extensive experience in enterprise-class systems design, application architecture and application development. Well-versed in current technology, understanding the role of IT/IS as it applies to business. Detailed oriented with a commitment to designing and developing quality solutions. Seeking team leadership role in a fast paced environment.

- Hardworking, conscientious, and highly skilled Software Development professional with a combination of strong technical, interpersonal, and management skills. Takes pride in leading by example and gives 100% to accomplishing goals and meeting deadlines. An outstanding problem solver who sees problems as challenges to be met and conquered. Thrives in fast-paced, technical environments. Seeking to join an organization where experience and education can be combined for mutual benefit.

- Senior database administrator with 10+ years experience in the support of corporate databases both locally and worldwide. Skilled at interfacing with internal customers, external vendors and working closely with various teams within the IT department to ensure effective software upgrades, migrations and installations. Seeking new opportunity to learn and build experience with a growing firm.

- Hardworking, conscientious, and highly skilled Software Development professional with a combination of strong technical, interpersonal, and management skills. Takes pride in leading by example and gives 100% to accomplishing goals and meeting deadlines. An outstanding problem solver who sees problems as challenges to be met and conquered. Thrives in fast-paced, technical environments. Seeking to join an organization where experience and education can be combined for mutual benefit.

- Senior information technology professional with proven experience in delivering technical solutions in diverse environments. Well developed reputation and consistent record in the area of infrastructure design, systems integration, applications, operations and security. Skilled in project planning, troubleshooting and providing technical support in a challenging and fast paced work environment.

Management

- A dynamic, results-oriented manager/administrator with expertise and experience in a T.Q.M/Continuous Quality Improvement environment. Comprehensive strengths in strategic planning and the management of change, systems analysis, project and financial management, and program evaluation. Superior interpersonal skills as exhibited through the coordination and negotiation/mediation of multiple projects/assignments. Seeking opportunities in organizations facing challenging comprehensive change.
- A highly skilled manager of diverse organizational functions. A strategic planner who takes initiative and is innovative, creative and meets goals. A leader who is a trainer, and team builder. A bottom line manager who increases productivity and organizational effectiveness. Highly organized with good communication and interpersonal skills.
- A progressive manager with extensive experience and diversified background. Highly motivated and innovative combined with excellent people and presentation skills. Results-oriented and demonstrated versatility in achieving organizational goals.
- A senior manager for over 20 years, in buying, marketing and human resources. Expert communicator and motivator. Imaginative, pioneering business attitude with a pragmatic approach to constraints and opportunities.
- An experienced general management and plant operations professional effective at organizing and directing production/profit centres in a participatory management environment. Goal-oriented with excellent communication and leadership skills complemented by a working knowledge of financial reports and strong technical abilities in the food industry. Career objectives are management opportunities in food and related industries.
- Seasoned general manager with a successful background in manufacturing and customer service and a reputation for achieving results. Proven strengths in the management of multiple sites and technical teams. Strategic thinker and creative troubleshooter who can quickly identify problems and oversee the implementation of practical solutions. Skilled leader with ability to develop and motivate strong managerial teams. Seeking new opportunities in a challenging environment.

Marketing

- An Entrepreneur with more than 15 years' experience focused on Marketing and Sales. Key elements of expertise are in achieving simultaneous maximization of market share and profitability, excellent interpersonal and communication skills and superior team-building talent. Hands-on professional who enjoys the challenge of an aggressive results-oriented total quality environment.
- Accomplished marketing and visual merchandising professional with extensive experience and expertise in the management of large and small scale retail enterprises. Superior strengths in aggressive sales techniques, dynamic marketing, power visual merchandising and quality customer service dedicated to bottom line profitability and accountability. Seeking challenge in a sales and marketing, or retail opportunity.
- Achievement driven marketing specialist with well developed market planning skills, resourceful problem solving expertise and a proven track record in sales. Hands-on professional who enjoys the challenge of a results-oriented environment. Seeking a leadership opportunity to utilize marketing and business expertise to meet and exceed corporate objectives.
- Dynamic marketing and advertising professional with experience in multi-level coordination and presentation in new product development. Proven operations manager possessing consumer driven business expertise. Achievement-oriented and bottom line focused. Seeking new and challenging opportunities.
- Professional manager with a solid background in marketing, transportation, quality control and processing. Self-motivated to provide innovative answers to complex problems in a low risk/low margin industry. Seeking opportunity to focus skills and expertise in a challenging environment.
- Professional marketing executive with proven track record in sales and management in a fast paced customer service environment. Young, open minded leader who believes all activities revolve around looking after the customer. Enthusiastic individual interested in meeting new challenges.

Non-profit Management

- A results-driven community organizational Executive Director with key strengths in the management of both professional and lay staff in all aspects of advocacy, promotion and fund raising. Possesses the ability to portray the needs of the organization to the population at large. Seeking challenges to utilize skills and expertise in a community setting.
- Experienced professional with key strengths in organizational management and significant leadership. Accomplishments in volunteer coordination, training, and specialized research. Self-motivated, analytical thinker with effective and strong interpersonal skills. Seeking challenging opportunities to utilize skills and strengths.
- Enthusiastic, self-directed and innovative team player with proven track record of accomplishments in business development and project coordination. Strong customer service orientation complemented by bottom line focus. Dedicated to seeking opportunities to utilize organizational skills in a people-oriented environment.
- Highly energetic, people-oriented individual with excellent organizational and administrative qualities. Demonstrated and proven strengths in research and development of ground level projects, action -oriented problem solving skills, refined reflective skills and creative thinking.
- Project-oriented visionary and highly energetic professional sales manager and fund-raiser with a keen sense of the marketplace. Demonstrates high level of competence in communicating, promotional advertising, training programs, introducing customer appreciation procedures, developing revenue and operating budgets, trouble shooting and team building.
- Resourceful, versatile executive with eight years of senior management experience, proactive marketing, and a demonstrated ability to get the job done. An innovative achiever with excellent interpersonal skills and who thrives on teamwork and a challenge.
- Self-motivated bilingual professional with key strengths in management, coordination training in multi-cultural settings. Results-oriented catalyst with strong problem solving, negotiation and decision making skills, complemented by extensive sales and marketing within a non-profit environment.

Operations / Project Management

- A General Manager experienced in managing operations, finances and personnel within the commercial and retail sales environment. With demonstrated expertise in hiring, training, motivating and terminating staff, market identification and sales projections, general budget preparation, and overall financial management to ensure the best possible bottom line results. A highly self-motivated individual, who enjoys the challenges of problem solving, being a team leader, implementing new ideas in business, and providing a superior customer service.
- An innovative operations and customer service professional, with the skills required to successfully implement change in a dynamic environment. Strong leadership, analytical and communication skills combined with a decisive problem solver. Seeking an opportunity to make a significant contribution in a team environment.
- Conscientious, responsible, hands-on professional with extensive experience in production management, sales, engineering and quality assurance. People and customer-oriented, humanistic approach to problem solving with keen ability to develop trust in an encouraging and supportive environment. Strong team orientation with well developed customer service skills.
- Experienced operations and production professional with keen ability to analyze and implement new ideas in retail and plant settings. Extensive track record in training and development with demonstrated ability to coordinate operations in a fast paced environment.
- Experienced project management and building planning professional possessing demonstrated organizational abilities. Proven skills in project coordination and crisis management. Accomplished in providing on time and on budget project completions. Self-motivated analytical thinker with strong communication skills.
- Professional manager with responsible experience in project management, systems improvement and computerized accounting. Strong team builder with system skills who effectively solves problems and implements solutions.

Policy Analysis

- Accomplished professional with key strengths in fields of economics and political science complemented by a solid foundation in the analysis of legal and legislative issues. Energetic and thorough with excellent interpersonal skills for participation in a team environment, seeking challenges which provide for key goals in political, economic and social change.
- Experienced, professional manager specializing in social policy and research. Committed to integrity, pursuing a vision and turning complex problems into opportunities. Strong analytical problem solving, negotiation and decision making skills with extensive Canadian and International experience in Health and Rehabilitation. Seeking continued progressive research, policy and academic challenges.
- Highly motivated administration manager, with specific expertise and proven experience in the examination, design and implementation of Business Accounting Systems for Manufacturing, Contracting, Retail and Service Industries. Trained in Legislation and Policy on Provincial Tax Statutes and Federal Taxation.
- Skilled professional with fourteen years of program management and policy development experience within a multi-disciplinary environment. Creative and innovative manager with an intuitive ability to complement an organization's changing environment. Seeking an opportunity to meet challenges while contributing to the bottom line.
- A senior corporate executive with valuable experience in enterprise-wide policy analysis, initiation, creation and implementation and vast knowledge and skills working with Ministerial and senior political officials with the expectation of producing challenging deliverables. Keen business acumen, extensive experience and expertise in effectively building relationships with a diverse group of people through professional, political and community activities to assemble high level solutions. Strong negotiator and decision maker with excellent interpersonal and communication skills as demonstrated in assisting members to meet their mandate.

Retail Management

- Agriculture graduate with extensive farm management experience as well as managing operations, finances and personnel in the commercial and retail sales setting. Demonstrated expertise in human resource management, general budget preparations, sales projections and overall financial management which achieved top customer service. A highly self-motivated individual who enjoys the challenge of problem solving, implementing new ideas in business and works effectively on boards and committees. An active participant in many community organizations and clubs.

- Experience gained by 18 years of management in several areas of the retail sector. Effective in maintaining and controlling all costs relative to budget projections. Committed to developing a team dedicated to sales volume without compromising customer services or satisfaction. Seeking a sales intensive position where my skills with people, both customer and staff, can be used to their full potential.

- Extensive administrative management experience working within retail and warehouse environments. Strong financial skills with demonstrated marketing skills and experience. Proven initiative, with the ability to motivate staff in order to effectively achieve objectives in a given time frame.

- Fluently bilingual hands-on general manager with extensive experience in the retail sector. Demonstrated expertise in operations analysis, systems development, loss prevention, risk management recruitment and training. Dedicated to maintaining customer service without compromising profitability.

- Retail professional with a positive, success-oriented attitude complemented by thirteen years of experience in management and supervision of daily operations and financial planning. Skilled in meeting management challenges of a retail chain of multi-geographical locations.

- Seasoned administrative manager with extensive experience obtained within a retail environment. Excellent financial knowledge of planning, analysis, and evaluating plans. Dedicated team player with proven interpersonal skills applied in accomplishing department and company objectives.

Sales and Marketing

- A dedicated and conscientious sales manager with a proven track record and extensive management background in recruiting, negotiation, interpersonal and communication skills. Excellent interpersonal strengths with highly developed leadership qualities. Well organized team player with the ability to work independently.
- A professional with more than 20 years' experience focused primarily on purchasing, customer relations, sales development and administration. Particularly recognized for strengths in planning, organization, establishing cooperative and productive relationships and a substantial and diversified knowledge base. Hands-on administrative manager, resourceful, proficient in project management and demonstrates grace under pressure.
- A seasoned marketing and sales professional with 10 years' progressive experience in the food production and service industry. A multidimensional manager with superior strengths in cooperatively maximizing sales and staff potential, market analysis, and regional distribution strategies, creative training programs and effective team building. Hands-on professional who enjoys the challenge of an aggressive, results-oriented total quality environment.
- Agriculture graduate with extensive farm management experience as well as managing operations, finances and personnel in the commercial and retail sales setting. Demonstrated expertise in human resource management, general budget preparations, sales projections and overall financial management which achieved top customer service. A highly self-motivated individual who enjoys the challenge of problem solving, implementing new ideas in business and works effectively on boards and committees. An active participant in many community organizations and clubs.
- Creative sales and marketing professional with significant management experience in challenging, fast paced environments. Highly motivated with strong leadership and administrative strengths supported by good communication and public relations skills. Keen business development sensitivity including evaluation and goal setting for bottom line performance in start-up opportunities. Exceptional analytical skills that help strengthen a successful win/win negotiation style.

Social Services Management

- Accomplished professional possessing executive level expertise in social service delivery. Skilled legal practitioner with ability to address practical issues with empathy. Demonstrated skills in planning and management, grant writing, advocacy, mediation, program design, budgeting and research.
- Excellent skills and abilities in crisis, stress and anger management including assessment, counselling and client monitoring.
- Experienced human relations professional with key strengths in conflict resolution, mentoring and group facilitation. A solution-centered and sensitive counsellor, great communicator, and team player. Dedicated to the personal development of individuals and groups. Seeking employment in a personal, professional and disciplined environment.
- Good working knowledge of a number of key justice department and social services programs including the Fine Option Program, the Community Service Order Program, Parole Supervision and Community Assessments.
- Proven proficiency in crisis management and conflict resolution through effective use of issues identification, mediation and sound decision making skills.
- Seasoned crisis counselling and mediating professional with excellent skills in problem identification, analyses and conflict resolution. Addresses advocacy issues with a humanistic management approach.
- Significant knowledge of the corrections system with the ability to provide assessment, counselling and treatment referral for men and women involved with drug and alcohol abuse.
- Skilled in family violence and abuse counselling including sexual, mental, physical and chemical, providing individual, family and group counselling.
- Solid foundation and working knowledge of vocational rehabilitation, health, disabilities, child welfare, and employment equity.
- Solid teamwork skills with the ability to work with a multi-disciplinary team of professionals to develop, deliver and evaluate social service programming.

Technical/Manufacturing/Engineering

- A hands-on manager with more than 20 years' experience in technical and engineering organizations. Knowledgeable in mechanical, electrical, hydraulic and pneumatic systems, as well as manufacturing tooling, equipment and quality assurance, Experienced in local, national and international government procurement practises. Conducted international marketing activities, market research and business development assessment for engineered products and services.
- Extensive and diverse background in product management within the construction industry. Effective in maintaining cost control relative to budget projections. Committed to teamwork in a departmental setting.
- Progressive manufacturing operations professional with a strong management style, enhanced by technical competence, financial acumen and successful project leadership. Hands-on manager who enjoys the challenge of problem solving in a results-oriented, total quality environment. Seeking to participate as a member of a dedicated and skilled management team in an organization and be part of a success story.
- Progressive manufacturing operations professional with a strong management style, enhanced by technical competence, financial acumen and successful project leadership. Hands-on manager who enjoys the challenge of problem solving in a results-oriented, total quality environment. Seeking new operational challenge.
- Seasoned professional with superior skills and expertise in prototype mechanical design. Extensive, and successful research and supervisory experience with solid reputation for innovation and productivity. Qualified and comfortable working with manufacturing and marketing professionals to develop commercially viable products. Seeking continued creative design challenges.
- Results oriented senior engineering professional with 20+ year's experience; a unique blend of specialized skills as a plant engineer, engineering sales professional, general management with the ability to provide formal industrial focused education. Superior project management skills with a high level of organizational skills for developing and implementing complex projects. Strong analytical problem solving, negotiation and decision making skills; seeking highly responsible management challenges with a growing organization.

Training And Development Business Leadership

- Creative and innovative trainer and facilitator with intuitive ability to assist organizations in their changing environments. Skilled professional with fourteen years of program management and policy development within a multi-disciplinary field. Sensitive to the effects change will have socially, economically and environmentally.
- Innovative training and development professional with project management background. Proven expertise in competency based training, adult education and community development. Strong interpersonal, problem solving and teamwork skills gained and demonstrated through challenging work projects and extensive community and board activities.
- Accomplished cross cultural professional with superior strengths in training, counselling and management. Bottom line focused, well organized and action-oriented problem solver who thrives on innovative challenges. Excellent interpersonal skills in diverse working environments. Seeking challenges utilizing comprehensive skills and expertise.
- Self-motivated bilingual professional with key strengths in management, coordinating and training in multi-cultural settings. Results-oriented catalyst with strong problem solving, negotiation and decision making skills, complemented by extensive sales and marketing skills within a training environment.
- A nursing professional with a strong background in clinical and classroom teaching. Extensive experience in curriculum development, program planning, implementation and evaluation. Well organized, high energy professional seeking an opportunity in nursing education.
- Innovative, proactive and dynamic leader skilled in communicating throughout the organization. Experienced professional manager specializing in program design, project management and organizational development. Looking for challenges utilizing skills to contribute to an organization.

Résumé Examples

A select number of résumés are provided for you to demonstrate that the transferable résumé style can be applied to most professions. Note that page one of each résumé is similar but that the following pages and sections are then customized to meet the need of the individual writer.

Financial Management

Accountant

Barbara J. Bowes
48 Résumé Drive, Winnipeg, Manitoba, R0X 3B6
Phone: 1-809-224-9993 Email: you@youraddress.com

A chartered accountant with over 10 years' experience as controller, manager and financial consultant to businesses in the public and private sectors. Highly motivated and innovative with exceptional skills in analyzing, developing and implementing computer systems. Seeking an opportunity that welcomes a strong work ethic and commitment to corporate goals.

Professional expertise

- Extensive experience in the preparation and analysis of monthly and year end financial statements, annual budgets, quarterly forecasts, cash flow projections and capital requirements.
- Demonstrated bottom line accomplishments through solid supervision and management of financial reporting and control functions in a multi-million dollar operating environment.
- Excellent strengths in computer-assisted financial planning, analysis and the design of customized spreadsheets in the area of profit plan development, capital plans, cost analysis, and financial statement preparation.
- Well developed skills in capital resource investment, audit and evaluation with experience in the development of replacement and preventative maintenance programs.
- Solid interpersonal and human resource management strengths with the capacity to work with a variety of people in a dynamic, supportive and participative work environment.
- Good oral and written communication skills; able to provide well thought out summaries and reports that are easily understood and logically presented.

Accomplishments

- Administered an annual budget of $30.5 million, achieving budgetary surpluses each year while also significantly expanding business.
- Coordinated the computer implementation for the financial reporting and management of information requirements for six national corporate subsidiaries.
- Designed, developed, negotiated and implemented an electronic payment system resulting in more efficient payment and improved company receivables.
- Pursuant to the sale of company to a large multinational, redesigned the management reporting, budgeting and financial statement presentations to comply with the new parent requirements.

Education/Professional Development

Bachelor of Commerce, University of Northern Saskatchewan, 1982

Total Quality Management for Controllers,
Canadian Manufacturers Association and University of Alberta

Canadian Investment Finance, Canadian Securities Institute, Toronto

Creating a highly motivated finance team, Community College

Work History

Controller, Canadian Express, Winnipeg, 1990 - present

Assistant Controller, Canadian Express, Winnipeg, 1998-1990

Assistant Controller, St. James Cartage and Storage, 1985 - 1988

Financial Management

Finance Executive

Barbara J. Bowes
48 Résumé Drive, Winnipeg, Manitoba, R0X 3B6
Phone: 1-809-224-9993 Email: you@youraddress.com

Senior corporate finance executive with keen business acumen, extensive experience and expertise in strategic financial planning and reporting, treasury and banking, risk management, accounting, management information systems and human resource compensation benefits. Strong negotiator and decision maker with excellent interpersonal and presentation skills; seeking executive career challenges in a sophisticated customer service and results-oriented environment.

Professional Expertise

- Highly developed organizational, administrative and financial management strengths utilizing continuous quality improvement for the efficient and effective management of office structure, day-to-day operations including systematizing allocation of resources and monitoring workload.

- Corporate-level financial and economic analysis skills and experience in major acquisitions, divestitures and capital expenditure decisions.

- Excellent treasury and banking expertise including negotiating and structuring corporate credit, foreign exchange and interest rate risk management, cash flow management and related policy development.

- Exceptionally creative with substantial ability and success in the identification of customer and business trends, the identification and exploitation of market opportunities, conducting competitive analysis and the initiation and design of co-ventured partnerships.

- Demonstrated ability to develop staffing, compensation and benefit plans for the integration of human resources with other corporate business plans resulting in overall productivity improvements and cost reductions.

- Effective and persuasive negotiation strengths with a deep appreciation of the quality and value a diverse group of internal and external customers holding wide ranging views.

- A calculating risk taker who implements creative practical solutions for profit and sales achievement for both company and clients resulting in mutual satisfaction and long term relationships.

Accomplishments

- Assumed the responsibilities of corporate controller for an extended period. Communicated with divisions and established report requirements, deadlines and issued monthly, quarterly financial statements, budgets and profit plans in a timely manner.
- Implemented a daily cash flow analysis allowing management to forecast monthly expenditures to minimize use of bank overdraft.
- Pursuant to the sale of the company to a large multinational, redesigned the management reporting, budgeting and financial statement presentations to comply with the new parent requirements.
- Prepared and maintained payroll records up to and including T-4 document preparation. Designed, implemented and monitored cash and financial controls.
- Successfully established and implemented cost control systems resulting in a 15% profit increase.
- Under personal leadership, directly contributed to achieving record profit during a downturn in the economy.

Professional/Community Leadership

Vice President, Finance Executives, Vancouver, 2008-2009

Professional of the Year Award, National Association of Finance Executives, 1992

Chair, Discipline Committee, Finance Executives, Vancouver, 1990-1994

Member, Professional Development/Examination Committees, Institute of Chartered Accountants, 1981-1989

Guest Lecturer, Management Studies, University of British Columbia, 1981-current

Employment History

Chief Financial Officer, Cassan Corporation, Vancouver, 1990-2009

Assistant to the Chief Financial Officer, Cassan Corporation, Vancouver, 1985-1990

National Controller, Johnson Western Equipment Distributors, Vancouver, 1981-1985

Education

Business Administration (MBA), University of Manitoba, in progress

Chartered Accountant, Manitoba Institute of Chartered Master of Accountants, 1980

Communications/Public Relations

Barbara J. Bowes
48 Résumé Drive, Winnipeg, Manitoba, R0X 3B6
Phone: 1-809-224-9993 Email: you@youraddress.com

Enterprising, innovative communications and public relations professional with significant project management skills for the management of major communications campaigns in both the private and public sector, Exceptional team leadership, organizational and motivational skills for the achievement of clearly defined goals and measurable results. Seeking an opportunity to become a key contributor in a team-oriented environment.

Professional Expertise

- Significant experience and expertise in all aspect of communications, public and media relations including television, radio and print media.
- Significant creativity for concept and implementation of unique and effective public relations and marketing strategies in multi-task, change oriented and time sensitive environments.
- Superior organizational expertise for project management of national and local events followed by the planning, coordination, implementation and follow through of strategies necessary for successful project completion.
- Detailed and results-oriented leadership drive complemented by a participative and flexible approach to team management.
- Excellent research strengths with skills in market trend analysis and the development of strategic plans to meet market needs.
- Outstanding presentation skills, experienced working with large and small groups.
- Action-oriented innovator able to meet time and budget targets by strategic analysis of possibilities, employing logic and ingenuity.
- Twenty years experience working in an international environment with an understanding of different cultures and communities for effective communication and well adapted messages.
- Excellent strategic organizational planning and coordination skills for projects, events and program initiation, staffing, start-up implementation and timely completion within limited budgets and resources.

Achievements

- Supervised all stages of television commercial production for a large Western Canadian Corporation, coordinated and managed all effort of advertising agencies and various production house resources.
- Managed the input of freelance resources in the development of marketing communications and advertising projects including graphic designers, printers, photographers, and audio and video production specialists.
- Created and implemented strategic communication packages including event planning, media relations and collateral materials development for public and private enterprise.
- Organized and coordinated logistics for public meetings and events including a highly successful rally for seniors that was instrumental in forcing a reversal in government policy.
- Facilitated communication and provided objective leadership between government, community, business and labour groups.

Work History

Writer/Producers, Dow and Dow Advertising, Winnipeg, 1990- current

Creative Supervisor, Carlton/Hall Productions, Toronto, 1980-1990

Creative Director, Print, Mint and Burkley Marketing, Toronto

Manager of Communications and Protocol, Backfield Corporation

Education/Professional Development

Applied Arts Diploma - Creative Communications, Local Community College, 1980

Report and Letter Writing

MacIntosh Levels 1, 2, 3

130

Engineer

Barbara J. Bowes
48 Résumé Drive, Winnipeg, Manitoba, R0X 3B6
Phone: 1-809-224-9993 Email: you@youraddress.com

A professional engineer with over twenty years' experience and extensive management expertise in diverse manufacturing and operating environments. Demonstrated proficiency in the integration of people and resources to maximize productivity and increase production.

Professional Expertise

- Strong organizational and administrative strengths for the development and implementation of operating and financial work plans.
- Demonstrated experience in human resources management complemented by well developed interpersonal skills and a proven track record in the establishment of positive working relations with all levels of personnel.
- Creative approach to problem solving with the ability to view a problem from several perspectives, develop alternative solutions.
- Extensive experience in the evaluation, selection, installation and commissioning of a wide variety of manufacturing equipment in diverse environments.
- Excellent project management skills with significant expertise in the management of diverse projects including identification of issues, planning, budgeting, implementation and monitoring for successful completion.
- Assertive and effective communication style; able to provide written and verbal summaries and reports that are easily understood and logically presented.
- Solid understanding of environmental assessment procedures with ability to manage the corporate requirements of a licensing process.

Accomplishments

- For over 15 years, successfully managed plant profit responsibility for a $45 million division of a multi-product international corporation. Managed 125 employees and oversaw all functional areas of operation including human resources management, sales, marketing, manufacturing, distribution, and cost control.
- Developed, implemented and led a Total Quality Management program resulting in an effective customer-oriented organization, which acted as the model for the present organization.
- Improved inventory control systems resulting in improved customer service through reduced back orders and reduced costs. Improved purchasing practises, shipping/receiving unit product costs.

Employment History

Plant Manager, Dominion Electronics, Montreal, 1980-2008

General Manager, Canadian Liquids Manufacturing, 1971-1980

Professional Development/Education

Certificate in Management (CIM), Canadian Institute of Management, 1974

Effective Supervision, Montreal Institute of Management

Frontline Leadership, Zenger-Miller

Workplace Health and Safety, Quebec Labour Council

Effective Interpersonal Skills, Xerox Learning Systems

Bachelor of Commerce (Honours), Concordia University

Bachelor of Arts (Business Administration), Quebec College

Food Services Manager

Barbara J. Bowes
48 Résumé Drive, Winnipeg, Manitoba, R0X 3B6
Phone: 1-809-224-9993 Email: you@youraddress.com

Results-oriented General Manager who thrives on the challenge of continuous improvement in a customer service environment. Proven skills in project management, training, recruitment and communication. Demonstrated expertise in operation analysis, systems development, loss prevention and risk management. Dedicated to maintaining and improving customer service without compromising profitability within a food services environment.

Professional Expertise

- Well developed customer service philosophy with proven skills in the development of award-winning service standards.
- Highly skilled in detailed and comprehensive analysis of financial information, inventory systems, training procedures and food preparation procedures.
- Demonstrated expertise in financial management and cost containment including budget determination and attainment, payroll procedures and controls, profit and loss analysis and waste minimization procedures.
- Human resource management skills including recruiting, employee training and development, performance procedures and employee relations.
- Strong organizational abilities for the development, implementation, coordination and management of business plans, marketing strategies, operational procedures and standards.
- Established proficiency in utilizing computer technology for the effective management of records, sales and costs.
- Participative management style with proven ability to achieve desired goals.
- Strong interpersonal skills with a demonstrated ability for effective communications.

Accomplishments

- Key member in the coordination of a new facility opening which achieved the lowest problem ratio of new openings for the restaurant chain.
- Redesigned a labour scheduling system to optimize labour hour apportionment. Increased service standards with no increase in operating costs.
- Following a detailed work analysis of time and employee allocation, instituted a strategy which reduced labour overtime 84% while maintaining customer service excellence.
- Designed and implemented management and employee training programs resulting in a hospitality award as well as an improvement of comprehension, knowledge, training consistency and overall employee satisfaction.
- Responsible for the management, training, development and coordination of a five person management team and a staff of 100 employees.
- Successfully operated a 250 seat, full service restaurant with consistently high achievement ratings for service, cleanliness, procedural integrity and guest service as determined by the corporate audit division.
- Conducted a review of facility maintenance costs, re-organized and restructured procedures and contractors, resulting in a savings of $20,000 within a twelve month period.

Work History

General Manager, Carlton Gardens Restaurants (Manitoba), 1994-2009

Unit Manager, Emma's Restaurants of Canada, 1988-1994

Assistant Manager, Don's Pizza Palace, 1980-1988

Professional Development/Education

Management Development Program, Carlton Gardens Restaurants

Advanced Leadership Skills, Leadership Institute of Manitoba

Inventory Management, Leadership Institute of Manitoba

Advanced Micro-Computers, Harvard Community College

Certified General Accountant

Bachelor of Arts, Geography

General Manager

Barbara J. Bowes
48 Résumé Drive, Winnipeg, Manitoba, R0X 3B6
Phone: 1-809-224-9993 Email: you@youraddress.com

Proven administrator and manager with excellent interpersonal and communication skills. A strong organizer and planner who is creative, innovative and entrepreneurial. Dedicated professional who thrives on challenge, possesses integrity and demonstrated initiative, professionalism and a positive attitude.

Professional Expertise

- Well developed strategic business planning, financial management and operational skills with proven expertise and accomplishments in the coordination and management of complex, multi-site businesses.
- Superior negotiation skills for the achievement of cost savings, profit targets, and profits.
- Participative management style with proven team building accomplishments complemented by excellent interpersonal skills resulting in the achievement of desired goals.
- Demonstrated success at setting objectives and achieving goals within a challenging, fast-paced environment.
- Experienced in human resources management including employee selection, evaluation, supervision and development.
- Excellent written and oral communication strengths; able to write clear and concise technical and management reports and make presentations.
- Solid customer service philosophy with a focus on customer satisfaction and the development of long term relationships with customer and suppliers.
- Excellent interpersonal skills; able to quickly develop the trust of others; approachable with an ability to maintain confidentiality.

Accomplishments

- Undertook strategic planning, as well as led a major corporate downsizing of a multi-site operation resulting in the seamless facilitation of layoffs and terminations.
- Designed, developed and implemented a new organizational structure which resulted in the improvement of operation and efficiency.
- Strategized and negotiated a strategic alliance with a competitor resulting in the collaboration of a new and highly successful corporate venture with the partnership continuing today.
- Using customer service expertise complemented by negotiation and communication strengths, was able to secure a large corporate client from a previously long term competitive relationship.

Work History

General Manager, Varsity Batteries, Sloan, Ontario, 1983- current

Assistant General Manager, Halcyon Turbo and Fuel, Downsview, Ont., 1977-1983

Branch Manager, Reno Equipment, Farnsworth, Ontario, 1966-1977

Education

Certificate in Management, Rowland Community College, Downsview

Top Quality Management, Rowland Community College, Downsview

Effective Speaking, Dale Carnegie

Health Care

Barbara J. Bowes
48 Résumé Drive, Winnipeg, Manitoba, R0X 3B6
Phone: 1-809-224-9993 Email: you@youraddress.com

Innovative, proactive and dynamic health care professional skilled in communicating throughout the organization. Experienced professional manager specializing in program design, project management and organizational development. Looking for challenges utilizing skills to contribute to an organization.

Professional Expertise

- Solid health care expertise for client health care assessments, and patient care education both within an institutional as well as an organizational work environment.
- Exceptional interpersonal and communication skills, sensitive to individual needs as they relate to group process and the goals of the organization.
- Skills in health program needs assessment, information analysis, program development, design and delivery at the patient and professional levels.
- Natural leader who can use persuasive communication to create win/win situations.
- Effective public relations skills with the ability to communicate concepts, and provide information at all organizational levels.
- Proficient at human resource and financial management in a multi-disciplinary work environment.

Professional Achievements

- Led and managed a private sector health care personnel agency with a client base of over 250, and a staff resource of 50.
- Successfully collaborated with a non-profit health agency and a professional association to design and implement the first foot care program with a primary focus on prevention and health education.
- Designed, developed, pilot tested and applied a community based initial health assessment tool which was modeled on a health promotion and wellness structure.

- Coordinated a community-based practicum experience for over 50 university nursing, pharmacy and dental hygiene students providing orientation, clinical supervision and student follow-up.
- Gathered and analyzed data on Pallative Care services in three provinces; authored a report and presented a set of recommendations which have now been integrated into provincial policy in two out of the three provinces.
- Initiated and developed a strong participative team management approach while simultaneously facilitating the integration of a total quality management problem solving resulting in obtaining a three year Accreditation Certificate.
- Initiated and guided an issues-oriented Community Health Practice Program which brought about increased community awareness and involvement in home health care involvement.

Employment History

General Manager, Health by the Hour Services, Ottawa ON., 1995 – 2009

Managing Director, Colburg Wellness Centre, Downsview, ON., 1990 – 1995

Clinical Instructors/Student Advisor, University of Downsview, 1989 – 1990

Planning and program analyst, Province of Ontario

Assisitant Director Of Nursing, St. Josephs on the Lake

Charge Nurse, Golden West Health Care Centre

Education/Professional Development

Master Of Business Administration, University of St. John's, 2009

Master Of Nursing, University of North Dakota

Bachelor Of Nursing, University of North Dakota

Professional/ Community Leadership

Invited Guest Speaker, Canadian Nursing Organizations

Invited Guest Speaker/ Lecturer, University of Downsview

Member, Health Education Practitioners of Canada

Director, Canadian Cancer Society

Health Services Management

Barbara J. Bowes
48 Résumé Drive, Winnipeg, Manitoba, R0X 3B6
Phone: 1-809-224-9993 Email: you@youraddress.com

Experienced, professional manager specializing in the health/service sector. Committed to integrity, pursing a vision focusing on solutions and turning complex problems into opportunities. Strong analytical problem solving, negotiation and decision making skills with extensive Canadian and International experience in Health and Rehabilitation. Seeking highly reputable management challenges.

Professional Experience

- Exceptional skills and innate ability to effectively lead and motivate professional staff towards a mission which targets organizational needs and produces significant positive change over time.
- High level of expertise in program planning, needs assessments, implementation design, delivery and evaluation.
- Broad human resource expertise and experience including recruitment, selection, organizational audits, program evaluation, policy development and review.
- Strong interpersonal and negotiation skills, effective communication to all levels including senior managers, government, volunteer boards and executive, consignors and colleagues. Equality strong in oral and written modes of communication.
- Solid foundation and working knowledge of health, rehabilitation and disability issues, child welfare, employment equity and vocational rehabilitation.
- Developing strengths in conflict management; able to facilitate front line group conflict sessions resulting in consensus decision making and resolution.
- Keen sensitivity to organizational issues, able to clarify and prioritize items for discussion.

Major Accomplishments

- Initiated needs assessments and feasibility studies and negotiated funds for local interest groups resulting in three community-based resource centres which have sustained and expanded over the past decade.

- Directed a research team to implement a needs assessment of a professional organization resulting in a 90% membership return rate.

- Directed a management team to implement a marketing strategy which resulted in a 50% increase in community inclusion activities within a four month period.

- Designed, implemented and managed group training programs which have served as models within the disabled community locally, nationally and internationally.

- Researched, developed, implemented and evaluated five pilot curriculum programs, supervised the revisions with the result that the programs were successfully implemented on an international basis.

Employment History

Curriculum Consultant, ATCC Human Service Agency, Winterton, British Columbia, 1993- 2009

Adjunct Facility, Mount Mantee College, North Dakota, Thinker Hari Prasaad College, India, University of Winterton, Garden Grove College, 1988-1993

Program Manager/Vocational Rehab Counsellor, Vocational Rehabilitation Services, Province of Saskatchewan, Saskatoon, 1979-1988

Educational/Professional Development

Ph.D., Community Health, University of British Columbia, 1991

M.S.W., Policy and Administration, University of Manitoba, 1985

Certificate, Rehabilitation Counselling, Manitoba, 1984

B.S.W., Industrial Social Work, University of Manitoba, 1978

Assorted skill development courses including *Non Violent Crisis Management, Stress Management, CPR, First Aid, Adult Learning Principles, Research Methodologies, Supervisory Skills and Time Management*

Human Resources

Barbara J. Bowes
48 Résumé Drive, Winnipeg, Manitoba, R0X 3B6
Phone: 1-809-224-9993 Email: you@youraddress.com

Human resource generalist with over three years experience in a fast paced manufacturing work environment. Excellent planning and organizational skills for the effective implementation of new programs and initiatives. Good training skills and experience, able to take responsibility for new employee orientation and exit interviewing. Seeking additional responsibility and new learning opportunities in the HR role.

Professional Expertise

- Solid academic background in human resources accompanied by additional inhouse training programs in effective report writing, conflict resolution and team building.
- Well developed human resource generalist skills with experience in new employee orientation, front line supervisory training and performance evaluation.
- Skilled in planning, preparing, interviewing potential candidates and preparing recommendations for line managers; good experience in reference checking and preparing onboarding materials.
- Clear understanding of the impact of absenteeism; developing effective consulting skills in early return to work and employee accommodation programming.
- Growing expertise in the management of employee benefits accompanied by participation in salary surveys and job evaluation.
- Results oriented professional who thrives on taking on and learning new tasks; willingly provides support to HR manager and front line supervisors.
- Developing leadership skill with experience in leading small specialized project teams to design and recommend program changes.
- Detail oriented with well developed writing skills; able to effectively participate in policy development and the writing of employee handbooks and training materials.

Accomplishments

- Led a team of 4 HR professionals to conduct focus groups of front line supervisors to evaluate the effectiveness of the corporate performance management system. Project resulted in numerous recommendations which were presented to HR management.
- Met with representatives of workers compensation board and followed their advice to make recommended changes to the early return to work program; was recognized by management as "employee of the month."
- Over a seven month time frame, reviewed the internal HR policy manual and identified several areas requiring revision; was assigned the task to revise and ensure policies were compliant with legislation.
- Participated in and became one of three professionals certified in an inhouse, "Results Centred Leadership" program.

Community/Professional Leadership

Member, Society for Human Resource Management

Member, Arlington Toastmasters Club

Volunteer, United Way Grand Forks

Education

PHR Candidate, Human Resource Certification Institute (HRCI)

B.Comm (HR major), American Intercontinental University

Certificate, Dale Carnegie Public speaking

Work History

HR Generalist, BusinessPro Software International

HR Generalist, City of Grand Forks, one year term

Student intern, City of Grand Forks, three months

Information Technology – Software Developer

Barbara J. Bowes
48 Résumé Drive, Winnipeg, Manitoba, R0X 3B6
Phone: 1-809-224-9993 Email: you@youraddress.com

Hardworking, conscientious, and highly skilled Software Development professional with a combination of strong technical, interpersonal, and management skills. Takes pride in leading by example and gives 100% to accomplishing goals and meeting deadlines. An outstanding problem solver who sees problems as challenges to be met and conquered. Thrives in fast-paced, technical environments. Seeking to join an organization where experience and education can be combined for mutual benefit.

Professional Expertise

- More than 15 years of experience leading all stages of SDLC. This included requirements definition, analysis, architecture, design, implementation, testing, risk management, deployment and support.
- Designed, developed and implemented solutions for Enterprise Architecture including Business Architecture, Data Architecture, Applications Architecture and IT Architecture.
- Extensive experience in analysis, design, and development of various Internet and Intranet applications and databases using Oracle, MS SQL, Delphi, Java, C#.
- Excellent knowledge and more than 5 years experience in Object Oriented Programming & Design (OOP & OOD).
- Excellent in-depth knowledge of PL/SQL and T-SQL with more than 5 years experience in designing and developing databases, writing stored procedures, triggers and complex queries, database performance tuning and optimization.
- More than 9 years experience in developing Client/Server and Win32 applications and extensive experience in Java (J2EE, Servlets, JSP, JDBC).
- Excellent knowledge and strong experience using XML technologies and web technologies.
- Extensive experience in automating the process of software development: creating scripts for generating code for database objects, Delphi and Java classes, etc.

Accomplishments

- As senior developer, managed up to 15 technical resources such as DBA's, system analysts, developers and junior developers.
- Designed and developed communication interface with asynchronous data transmission in interaction with bank accounting system specialists. Implemented this interface in the authorization module using PL/SQL.
- Lead the collection of system requirements and designed and developed web-based UI using XML, XHTML, JavaScript and server-side application using Servlets.
- Designed an XML protocol for data exchange between GUI and database.
- Designed and developed APIs for integration of internal business systems with external systems and wrote the technical API specifications.
- Lead the design and development and successful implementation of a custom developed inventory management system using Java/J2EE and Oracle.

Employment History

Senior Developer (Contract), ABC Telco, June 2005 - Present

Senior Programmer/Analyst, Midsar Software LTD. May 2002 – May 2005

Programmer Analyst, First Global Financial Services Inc., July 2000 – April 2002

Junior Programmer, Greenboro Development Inc., Sept 1998 –June 2000

Professional Development/Educational Background

Certificate, Project Management, PMI, 2007

Certificate, Effective Business Communication Skills, 2005

Certificate, Sun Certified Web Component Developer (SCWCD), 2002

Certificate, Sun Certified Java 2 Programmer (SCJP), 2002

Bachelor of Science, Computer Sciences, 1998

Information Technology – Solutions Architect

Barbara J. Bowes
48 Résumé Drive, Winnipeg, Manitoba, R0X 3B6
Phone: 1-809-224-9993 Email: you@youraddress.com

Experienced professional IT Solutions Architect with 20 years extensive experience in enterprise-class systems design, application architecture and application development. Well-versed in current technology, understanding the role of IT/IS as it applies to business. Detail oriented with a commitment to designing and developing quality solutions. Seeking team leadership role in a fast paced environment.

Professional Expertise

- Extensive experience as a Solutions Architect at the enterprise level in designing systems and solutions to meet the business need of the organization; demonstrated expertise in database design, development and training with all database technologies.

- Solid background in web-based application design and development, user-experience design, operational support and project management at the enterprise level.

- Ten years experience designing Oracle-based solutions for large high technology corporations. Technical and functional proficiency with the Oracle Applications suite of products.

- Quick to learn with the ability to work in a team environment as well as independently. Strong people skills coupled with strong sense of ethical behavior and commitment.

- Self-motivated, client-oriented individual who has excellent communication skills and works well independently as well as on a team. Strong mentorshipability.

- Practical experience with the following technologies:

  Java/J2EE, Visual Basic, Perl, XML, C/C++, Python, HTML, JavaScript, Adobe Flex,UML Modelling.

  Vignette Portal and V7 CMS, Stellent CMS, Fatwire CMS.

  Oracle CoreID, Sun One LDAP.

  Oracle DB, mySQL, PostgreSQL, Apache and Zope.

  Solaris, Windows NT/2000/XP, Linux.

Accomplishments

- Senior Architect responsible for the lead role in defining, planning and executing strategic, IT-focused business application development initiatives.
- Managed a staff of 6 IT technologists with duties that included recruiting, workload management, general administration, training and development.
- As Solutions Architect, participated in IT due diligence processes for mergers and acquisitions; role included interviewing the target company's IT staff, auditing and inventorying computer systems including business applications, middleware, and hardware infrastructure.
- Successfully engaged as Solution Architect for many projects which involved working with the business and IT stakeholders to design user experience, create system requirements, conduct architecture design, systems and application design, acceptance test plans, and performance/capacity planning.
- Provided vision and technology guidance to the business and development teams related to portal, content management and identity management on the web.
- Acted as trusted advisor to senior management for strategic planning and short-term tactical issues. Participated in strategic planning and management of an IT program of more than $25M annually.
- Designed and architected the company's web portal and content management solutions. As the Technical Architect, Team Lead and project manager for several IT development projects.

Employment History

Senior Solution Architect, XYZ Inc., June 2005 - Current

Senior Delivery Manager, ABC Inc., April 2001 - May 2005

Senior Analyst, 123 Ltd., January 1996 - April 2001

Programmer Analyst, Design Architects Inc, April 1988- Dec. 1995

Professional Development/Educational Background

Consultant Certification, Rational Unified Process, Rational University, 2005

Certificate, The Workplace Leader, 1995

Certificate, Admin/Developer Training, 1994

Certificate, TCP/IP Network Administration, 2001

Information Technology – Database Administrator

Barbara J. Bowes
48 Résumé Drive, Winnipeg, Manitoba, R0X 3B6
Phone: 1-809-224-9993 Email: you@youraddress.com
Barbara J. Bowes, B.Sc., BA

Senior database administrator with 10+ years experience in the support of corporate databases both locally and worldwide. Skilled at interfacing with internal customers, external vendors and working closely with various teams within the IT department to ensure effective software upgrades, migrations and installations. Seeking new opportunity to learn and build experience with a growing firm.

Professional Expertise

- Strong technical specialist skills, knowledge and experience in database administration including full life-cycle data architecture, logical and physical database design, data modeling, implementation, and administration within a Unix production environment.
- Strengths in the planning, installation, configuration and administration of multiple databases including skills in Oracle 11g/10g/9i databases, SQL, PL/SQL script writing, SQL tuning, ETL scripting and data refreshes: additional working knowledge of Sybase and Perl scripting.
- Experience in dealing with data confidentiality and security; skilled at developing policies and monitoring compliance to ensure security and confidentiality.
- Strengths in the oversight of all system maintenance activities including the installation and support of primary client programs.
- Skilled at writing application manuals, training users and developing standardized programming and data documentation procedures relevant to corporate data system needs.
- Able to play a key role in researching and recommending purchase of new hardware and software requirements to support database operations, data/project archives and disk maintenance.
- Well developed team leadership skills with a particular knack for identifying and developing junior level professional staff.
- Excellent communication and interpersonal skills; acknowledged for facilitation and business planning and financial management expertise.
- Well respected member of the management team with extensive experience in planning.

Accomplishments

- Led the database administration team in a business process re-engineering project that resulted in the successful integration of new desktop applications company wide.
- Designed and developed a database infrastructure that essentially re-engineered the entire corporate budgeting process; project was completed on time and under budget.
- Designed a departmental database recovery plan that was subsequently adopted corporate wide; received recognition and reward from company president.
- Designed and developed the corporate web application for the successful initiation into e-business solutions.
- Successfully grew the administration team from one performer to five staff; recognized by company for customer service.

Professional leadership

Chairman, Corporate Oracle Users Group, 2005-current

Volunteer, Corporate United Way Campaign

Education

Oracle Certified Master, Oracle 9I Database Administrator

Bachelor of Science, Computer Science, University of Guelph, Ontario

Bachelor of Arts, Psychology and Political Science, Athabasca University

Work History

Senior Database Administrator, Canada Safeway, Calgary

Database Administrator, Baker, Baker and Forbes, Vancouver

Database Administrator, Manulife Financial, Seattle

Marketing

Barbara J. Bowes
48 Résumé Drive, Winnipeg, Manitoba, R0X 3B6
Phone: 1-809-224-9993 Email: you@youraddress.com

Achievement driven marketing specialist with significant market planning skills, resourceful problem solving expertise and a proven track record. Creative, broad scoped strategic thinker with strong presence and keen abilities in trend analysis, customer needs identification and marketing program development. Seeking the challenge of a results-oriented environment.

Professional Expertise

- Exceptionally creative with substantial ability and success in the identification of customer and business trends, the identification and exploitation of market opportunities, conducting competitive analysis and the initiation and design of coventure programming.
- Skilled in strategic planning for corporate marketing and sales programming, complemented by a strong personal customer service and customer satisfaction philosophy.
- Strong leadership and administrative strengths for multi-million dollar budgetary responsibilities and line staff management with excellent interpersonal and human resource management skills.
- Considerable strengths in effective human resource management, recruitment, selection, training, motivating and performance evaluation.
- Significant oral communication and presentation skills for direct sales solicitation, sales presentations and internal staff training and development.
- A proven track record of working with a variety of people in dynamic, supportive and participative work environment.
- Very strong coding and debugging skills, can easily understand code written by others.
- Strong analytical, interpersonal, and communication skills and a good team player capable of working in a team or independently.

Accomplishments

- Created and implemented a computerized territory account planning system which facilitated the tracking, analysis and planning of specific geographic market plans and in turn the annual market plan.
- Developed, launched, coordinated and implemented a loyalty rewards retail program, which resulted in a card member base of approximately 50,000 and a retail/wholesale associate group in excess of 100 businesses in both urban and rural areas.
- As one of five key members of a national senior management committee, redefined the organizational structure, developed, directed and implemented national sales operations, annual marketing programs to support $54 million in sales, national employee incentives and development programs.
- Identified an ex-agent's move to a competitor, performed a successful search for a replacement agent, re-established direct account contact, developed and tracked market intelligence and thereby retained $1 million sales within a specified territory.
- Regained previously lost business with three strategic target accounts through the imitation of a key account sales effort resulting in a sales increase of $500,000.

Experience

General Manager, Royalty Rewards Limited Partnerships, Winnipeg

Regional Sales Manager, Reliance Lumber, Lawsdone, Manitoba

District Manager, Canadian Express, Manitoba

Senior Sales Supervisor, Commercial Sales Department, OilGas Ltd.

Professional Development/Education

Business Management Forum, Federal Business Development Bank

Selling Methods and Strategies, Cornerstone Management

Presentation Skills, Local Community College

Small Business Development

The Performance Edge

Professional Selling Skills

Bachelor of Commerce, Marketing, University of Alberta

150

Materials Management

Barbara J. Bowes
48 Résumé Drive, Winnipeg, Manitoba, R0X 3B6
Phone: 1-809-224-9993 Email: you@youraddress.com

Visionary materials management professional with a successful track record in high volume materials management. Efficient, results-oriented leader with strong human resources, financial and leadership skills. Seeking an opportunity to make a significant contribution in a fast paced challenging environment.

Professional Skills

- Maintaining a full set of financial records up to and including monthly and annual variance reports.
- Evaluating variance reports and making adjustments as required.
- Preparing and analyzing detailed feasibility studies and carrying out an action plan for project development.
- Excellent interpersonal skills to co-ordinate and participate in a team environment and achieve organizational goals.
- Effective control, policy development and evaluation of both perpetual and annual inventories.
- Liaison with all levels of management regarding policies, procedure and standards for the shipping and receiving of goods.
- Win/win negotiation approach for arriving at jointly agreed upon decision and bringing reconciliation to differing people both in a union and non union environment.
- Keen insights and ability to identify key problems and generate creative solutions.
- Creative and innovative in the delivery of professional development, and group facilitation processes.

Accomplishments

- Received, inventoried and annually supplied $25 million in medical-surgical supplies to over 50 satellite departments/agencies.
- Prepared implementation and supervised a department operating budget of $1 million; oversaw staff of 30.
- Using total quality management principles successfully reorganized and streamlined physical stock for faster access.
- Acted as a key team member in the computerization of a facility wide computerized inventory ordering system.

Work History

Assistant Director, Supply Services, Mountain Health Centre, Orillia, 1989-1994

Purchasing Manager, Parts Department, Kingston Transport, Orillia, 1982-1989

Head, Stores and Warehousing, Health and Welfare Canada

Inventory Supervisor, Health and Welfare Canada

Professional Development

Management programs: Extensive workshops and seminars in the areas of warehouse, supervisory, financial, materials management as well as the transportation of dangerous goods, hazardous chemicals and WHMIS.

Plant Manager

Barbara J. Bowes
48 Résumé Drive, Winnipeg, Manitoba, R0X 3B6
Phone: 1-809-224-9993 Email: you@youraddress.com

A committed, versatile and innovative plant manager with over twenty years experience in the management of manufacturing, sales, marketing and human resources. Demonstrated expertise in overall financial management, budget preparation and strategic planning; clearly focused on the bottom line.

Professional Skills

- A strong overall business background with a thorough understanding of all organizational functions and a demonstrated competence in managing them on a day-to-day basis.
- A positive, committed and adaptable management style that builds stability, loyalty and professional pride within an organization.
- Innovative and effect at improving production systems, work flow, productivity, product/service quality and individual/group performance.
- Accomplished human resource management strengths including recruitment, training, motivation, teambuilding and coaching.
- Talent for determining goals and objectives followed by the planning, organization, coordination and follow through necessary for successful project completion.
- Outstanding analytical abilities, able to package and communicate while still accounting for detail and inevitable exceptions.
- Experienced in policy and procedure formulation. Ability to plan, organize and follow through to implementation and control.
- Significant troubleshooting and crisis management skills; prepared to handle any given situation.
- Excellent interpersonal skills; able to quickly develop the trust of others; approachable with an ability to maintain confidentiality.

Accomplishments

- For over 15 years, successfully managed plant profit responsibility for a $45 million division of a multi-product international corporation. Managed 125 employees and oversaw all functional areas of operation including human resources management, sales, marketing, manufacturing, distribution, and cost control.

- Developed, implemented and led a Total Quality Management program resulting in an effective customer-oriented organization, which acted as the model for the present organization.

- Improved inventory control systems resulting in improved customer service through reduced back orders and reduced costs. Improved purchasing practises, shipping/receiving controls and overall inventory turnover.

- Expanded production capabilities to match 300% sales growth while at the same time reducing unit product cost.

Employment History

Plant Manager, Dominion Electronics, Montreal, 1980-2009

General Manager, Canadian Liquids Manufacturing, 1971-1980

Professional Development/Education

Certificate in Management (CIM), Canadian Institute of Management, 1974

Effective Supervision, Montreal Institute of Management

Frontline Leadership, Zenger-Miller

Workplace Health and Safety, Quebec Labour Council

Effective Interpersonal Skills, Xerox Learning Systems

Bachelor of Commerce (Honours), Concordia University

Bachelor of Arts (Business Administration), Quebec College

Social Services

Barbara J. Bowes
48 Résumé Drive, Winnipeg, Manitoba, R0X 3B6
Phone: 1-809-224-9993 Email: you@youraddress.com

Seasoned crisis counselling and mediation professional with excellent skills in problem identification, analyses and conflict resolution. Addresses advocacy issues with a humanistic management approach. Seeking opportunity in a challenging environment.

Professional Expertise

- Well developed interviewing, counselling, mediation and analytical skills; able to be understanding while quickly identifying client needs and issues, establishes client comfort and security, facilitates effective programs of problem resolution.

- Superior level of expertise and knowledge of community resources and support networks for education, self-improvement and family assistance which enables effective advocacy for children and families.

- Proven investigative and negotiation skills ensuring effective and appropriate crisis intervention.

- Empathetic listener with intuitive strength and rapid decision making ability.

- Solid working knowledge of client admission and release procedures including; processing, screening, interviewing, coordinating spaces, and working with external agencies to determine and meet client needs.

- Excellent interpersonal skills; able to quickly develop the trust of others; approachable with an ability to maintain confidentiality.

- Effective task orientation with ability to work as a team leader, able to delegate responsibility, ensure harmony, establish work priorities and schedules and address concerns of clients and staff members.

- Proficiency in report writing, public relations, staff scheduling, record keeping, program and policy development, implementation and evaluation.

Accomplishments

- Over a ten year period, successfully supervised and managed a diverse professional and non-professional staff of 50 during a difficult social services environment.
- Identified critical areas and developed appropriate policy, implemented, oversaw and evaluated policies and ensured policy manuals were regularly updated.
- Initiated, designed and implemented a quota list system enabling all agencies to prioritize their facility usage.
- Acted as a key team member to initiate, develop and implement a Cottage Intake concept within a one year timeframe.
- Initiated a continuous process improvement environment including conducting a needs assessment, designing the program and developing and training staff.

Professional Development/Education

Bachelor of Arts, Psychology, University of Canada

Certificate, Group Facilitation, Community Services Association

Working with Victims of Abuse

Stress Management

Non Physical Crisis Intervention

Assertiveness Training

Employment History

Staff Manager, Green Leaf Centre, Community Services, 1993-2008

Supervisor, Intake Cottage, Green Leaf Centre, Community Services, 1982-1993

Classroom Teacher, Arts and Crafts, City Oaks School Division, 1979-1982

Juvenile Counsellor, Summer Program, City Oaks School Division

156

Project Management

Barbara J. Bowes
48 Résumé Drive, Winnipeg, Manitoba, R0X 3B6
Phone: 1-809-224-9993 Email: you@youraddress.com

Experienced project management and building planning professional possessing demonstrated organization abilities. Proven skills in project coordination and crisis management. Accomplished in providing on time and on budget project completion. Self-motivated analytical thinker with strong communication skills.

Professional Expertise

- Excellent organizational and administrative skills with the ability to follow through on assignments to defined parameters.
- Assertive and effective communication and interpersonal skills. Reputation for providing easily understood and logically presented summaries and reports.
- Strong technical knowledge with superior strengths in planning, design and construction, stressing attention to accuracy and detail.
- Demonstrated ability to work with clients and associates at all staffing levels with a solid focus on customer service.
- Participative management style with proven teambuilding accomplishments.
- Solid understanding of national, provincial and civic building codes with ability to work effectively with jurisdictional authorities.
- Proven marketing ability to promote general and technical product information to facilitate material selection and specification.

Accomplishment

- Successfully managed a diverse array of projects varying degrees of complexity and size.
- Utilized professional project control methodology to ensure timely, efficient and economical work performance.
- Led and coordinated design and construction teams on high quality interior design-oriented projects. Achieved completion schedules well ahead of industry standards.
- Consistently provided leadership to ensure that project completions occurred on schedule by proactively solving delivery and installation problems.

Employment History

Manager, Architectural Team Inc., Winnipeg, 2003 – 2009

Project Coordinator, Ace Design and Development, 2002 – 2003

Project Manager/Estimator, Dominion Construction Ltd

Construction Coordinator, McLeods Architectural Group

Professional Development/Education

Certificate, Planning and Managing Working Drawings, University of Westgate

Certificate, Architectural Drawing, River Road College

Certificate, Computer Aided Drafting and Design, River Road Tech

Machine Drafting and Design, Westgage Technical School

Building Construction Technician, River Roach College

Research Scientist

Barbara J. Bowes
48 Résumé Drive, Winnipeg, Manitoba, R0X 3B6
Phone: 1-809-224-9993 Email: you@youraddress.com

A research and development professional who possesses excellent expertise in several areas of mathematical and physical sciences. Significant experience in academic research with a specialization in the application of mathematical methods to industrial issues. High proficiency in R & D project management rationalization, budget and proposal preparation, and technical liaison complemented by excellent interpersonal and organizational strengths.

Professional Expertise

- Skilled in the ability to develop conceptual framework and theories for the assessment of scientific technical problems an situations on a practical level.
- Significant strengths in numerical methods research in a number of research areas including radioactive transfer, gas ignition and biomass systems and fluid flow.
- Well developed scientific research methods in microwave remote sensing, density distribution and neutron transport tomography techniques.
- Significant laboratory strengths for the preparation, organization and coordination of test experiments involving interdisciplinary teams of physicists, chemists and engineers.
- Well developed writing skills; able to work with technical writing projects in English, French and German.
- Good interpersonal and communication skills for the collaboration and teamwork required in a scientific research team.

Reasearch Achievements

- Developed optimal method to produce charge profile of atmosphere by microwave remote sensing.
- Developed optimal numerical scheme to determine density distribution in rocks by sound travel time tomography.

- Developed more efficient numerical methods to determine flow regimes and void fractions in fluid flowing in pipes by gamma densitometers.
- Pioneered neutron transport tomography technique to determine flow regimes and void fractions in fluid flowing in fuel channels.
- Developed accurate and efficient methods to solve model equations describing radiative transfer in atmosphere.
- Developed accurate and efficient methods to obtain solutions and catastrophic points for gas ignition and biomass systems.
- Developed a new method to compute lower bounds to atomic binding energies.

Education

Ph.D. Physics, York University, Toronto, 1995

M.Sc. Physics, Queen University, Kingsfield, 1988

M.Sc. Physics, Agraa University, India, 1985

Employment History

Adjunct Professor, York University, Toronto, 1998 – present

Senior Scientist, Canadian Nuclear Research Centre, Pinawa, 1998 – 2006

Scientist/Lecturer, York University, Toronto, 1996 – 1999

Research Associate, University of Eastern Ontario

Professional Leadership

Publication: Over fifty research publications in refereed journals; presentation of papers at conference proceedings; publication of international reports, (list available)

Councilor, Centre for Mathematical Sciences, CNRC

University Liaison, University of Manitoba, York, Eastern

Television Host, Community Services Television

Sales

Barbara J. Bowes
48 Résumé Drive, Winnipeg, Manitoba, R0X 3B6
Phone: 1-809-224-9993 Email: you@youraddress.com

Results-oriented senior sales executive with a proven track record in the consumer products industry. Superior strengths in utilizing broad experience and creative strategies to facilitate successful completion of corporate objectives. Committed to associating with an organization which will profitably exploit my talents and energy.

Key Skills

- Extensive and diverse experience gained through effectively operating in over eight major retail trade classes, from boardroom to sales floor, to effectively implement and execute corporate selling plans.
- Dynamic, creative sales and marketing strategist who excels in working with the corporate team to generate realistic and achievable objectives.
- Superior strategic planning strengths in sales and marketing with the unique ability to conceive, design and implement company internal and external programs.
- Exemplary knowledge and application of the psychological principles of selling complemented by very strong interpersonal skill which confirm my abilities as a highly effective team leader, trainer and coach.
- A pro-active, enthusiastic and high energy approach not only to company goals, but also to the daily tasks needed to achieve them. Able to build enthusiastic employee participation.
- A calculating risk taker who implements creative practical solutions for profit and sales achievement for both company and clients resulting in mutual satisfaction and long term relationships.
- A keen profit awareness not only for initiating client programs which protect company profits and produce volume, but also by preparing and managing department budgets effectively with consent lookout for creative cost savings.

Accomplishments

- Envisioned a sales strategy for a stagnant, mature product line that increased annual volume from $1.4 million to $6 million and yielded significantly increased market share at the expense of competitors.
- Through an innovative sales approach, transformed a sales department operating expenses to become proportionate to sales performance, thereby protecting corporate vulnerability in difficult economic times and at the same time contributed more than $150,000 of previous annual expense to bottom line profit.
- Consistently achieved and regularly surpassed annual sales quotas with all companies within the budget resulting in consistent profitability. Frequent sales growth was achieved without benefit of new products in all major product line categories.
- Expertly managed national accounts and succeeded in significantly increasing their purchase of company product by millions of dollars annually. Achievement resulted in national awards.

Employment History

National Sales Manager, Ridley PenMaster Canada, Toronto, 1998 – present

National Sales Manager, Uniglue Limited, London, 1995 – 1998

Manager, Canadian Sales Development, Haritz Inc., 1991 – 1995

District Sales Manager, Dominion and Son, 1980 – 1991

Professional Development/Education

Managerial Grid, Scientific Systems, USA

Phone Power, Bell/Xerox

I.M.S. Instructor Program, Xerox

L.M.S., M.D.S. Program, Xerox

Professional Selling Skills

Dale Carnegie Public Speaking

Bachelor of Arts, Economics, University of Winnipeg

Sports

Barbara J. Bowes
48 Résumé Drive, Winnipeg, Manitoba, R0X 3B6
Phone: 1-809-224-9993 Email: you@youraddress.com

A challenge-oriented team player with a background as manager, trainer, coach and teacher in competitive sport and educational environments. Proven track record of success in leading and managing large sports events on a provincial and national basis. Seeking new career opportunities.

Professional Expertise

- A strong learner-centered trainer, coach and motivator.
- Experienced at identifying training needs, designing and implementing individual as well as group training programs and measuring results.
- Excellent verbal and written communication skills with experience in public speaking and promotional, education and policy writing.
- A resourceful administrator, effective at managing multi-level projects, defining organizational needs, improving structures and efficiently utilizing resources to achieve results.
- Well developed strengths in volunteer management with ability to recruit, train, motivate and supervise youth and adult volunteer teams.
- Good working knowledge of financial management, able to develop and manage an organizational and special events budget.

Accomplishments

Program Development

- Initiated and coordinated the development of a strategic plan for the Round Robin Rowing Club and Provincial Rowing Association; managed the successful organization and growth of both programs.
- Developed and coached numerous winning sport programs including 16 national titles which resulted in national recognition for team members.

Communication

- Wide experience researching and writing articles, reports, media releases, promotional and education materials.
- Designed and delivered train the trainer program and seminars to coaches, volunteers and conference attendees on a national basis.

Administration

- Liaised with government agencies and coordinated grants for the provincial association which increased by 40% over a three year period.
- Managed part-time and seasonal staff and volunteer coaches; developed job descriptions, hired, trained and evaluated.

Work History

Executive Director/Head Coach, Provincial Club Association, 2000 – 2009

National Program Manager, National Club Association, 1996 – 2000

Classroom Teacher, Jamestown High School, 1990 – 1995

Awards And Recognition

Coach of the Year, Provincial Sports Federation

Teaching Assistantship, University of Ottawa Valley

Athlete of the Year, Ottawa Valley High School

Education/Professional Development

Business Management Forum, Federal Business Development Bank

Masters of Arts, History, University of Ottawa Valley

Bachelor of Arts, History, University of Concord

Non-profit Management

Barbara J. Bowes
48 Résumé Drive, Winnipeg, Manitoba, R0X 3B6
Phone: 1-809-224-9993 Email: you@youraddress.com

An innovative, visionary leader with extensive experience with not-for-profit organizations. Highly organized with a proven track record of providing successful business direction and operation. Well developed expertise in strategic planning, financial management, organizational and staff development as well as marketing and fund-raising.

Professional Expertise

- Solid knowledge of board managed organizations with the ability to develop strong professional relationships with board members and volunteers.
- Superior leadership, planning and administrative management skills for the day-to-day operations of a $10 million organization with up to 35 staff.
- Good working knowledge of financial planning and accounting principles with demonstrated expertise in long term financial planning, annual budgeting, monitoring and reporting.
- Good understanding of marketing and sales concepts as they apply to non-profit service programs; able to identify client needs and develop/refine programs to meet these needs.
- Excellent communication and public relations skills; proven success in the design, development and implementation of newsletters, program brochures.

Accomplishments

- As a newly appointed Executive Director, conducted an organizational review and restructured the organization, thus improving the overall operation and efficiency.
- Facilitated and oversaw the design, development and implementation of polices in key operational areas such as personnel, administration, financial investments, board relations and board protocol.
- Led the task force on Total Quality management and applied procedures and tools to the organization resulting in seven teams in operation within one year and significant operating improvements.

Employment History

Executive Director, British Columbia Cultural Centre, 1999 – present

Assistant Executive Director, Saskatchewan Historical Association, 1995 – 1999

Program Management Specialist, Victoria Art History Centre

Community/Professional Leadership

Chair, UNICEF, British Columbia,

Chair, Fund-raising Committee, British Columbia

Executive Co-Chair, Junior League of Victoria

Member, Board of Directors, Victoria Rehab Housing

Chair/Coordinator, Community Association of Food Banks

Exhibition Coordinator, Festival of Arts Communities

Education/Professional Development

Marketing for Non-profit Associations, UBC

Accounting Systems for Non-profit Associations, UBC

Arts Policies and Institutions, British Council of the Arts

Problem Solving and Decision Making, Canadian Learning Systems

Diploma in Social Communications

Master of Art History